I Pledge Allegiance to God

What the Founders Write, Say and Pray about God

by

Barbara Schenkel

Xulon Elite

I Pledge Allegiance to God
What the Founders Write, Say and Pray about God
by Barbara Schenkel

Printed in the United States of America.

ISBN 9781498448376

www.xulonpress.com

Dedication

This book is dedicated to my dad, Richard Schenkel, who loved and taught history and brought our country's Founders to life for his students and family.

Acknowledgements

I give thanks for all the persons on my journey of writing this book who have given of their time to share a word of encouragement, say a prayer, or give a word of knowledge in support. This includes people I met on the street, in the grocery store, in the library, at family gatherings, at church, in my travels around Phoenix.

Special thanks to Rev. Fred and Jenny Mast, and to all the members and friends of Sunrise United Methodist Church who attended classes I taught on the "Prayers of Colonists, Clergy and Founders." You gave of your time and enthusiasm to attend and comment on class lessons I put together. With Rev. Fred Mast's encouragement, the lessons were researched, planned and classes ongoing during his pastorate at the church.

Thanks to Pastor Neil Leftwich who was pastor at Sunrise UMC ten years ago when I visited the church and asked, "What do you need help with?" His answer, "The prayer ministry."

With Pastor Neil's support, our prayer ministry program expanded. Without numerous prayer warriors who have faithfully prayed over the years, none of these classes or this book would have come to reality.

Thanks to Bobbie Rodriquez from Xulon Press who not only gave me the title for the book, but whose wonderful insight helped me focus on how to organize all the research information at hand. A *God moment* indeed!

Thanks to the staff at the Phoenix Public Library who were always helpful in finding books and items needed for my research.

Thanks to my dear friend, Betty Long, who agreed to proofread the text of this book and gave timely clarifications needed. Thanks to Deb and Dan Goebel and Donna Price for further reviews of the text.

Thanks to my parents, Richard and Mildred, who saw to it I attended church as a child and teenager. To my mom who taught me Bible stories as a youngster and to my dad who taught us all such inspiring history from the founding of our country.

Endorsements

As one who grew up sitting at my father's knee, longing and loving to hear the stories of past generations, Barbara Schenkel, in the pages of her new book, brings alive the stories and the lives of the courageous men and women who often risked it all and who were so instrumental in creating the legacy of this great land we so love and call America. Barbara has such incredible insight and knowledge, and is a remarkable writer, teacher and orator of history and religion coupled with a deep and abiding love for God and her faith. Her hunger and her passion for learning and sharing these timeless and critical pieces of history, while also bringing such enlightenment of the deep spirituality that so many of the founders possessed, is so important in a day and age in which our American heritage and history is in great danger of being lost and forgotten forever. I love how Barbara tells the story in the present tense and from the perspective of an intimate and personal conversation with God, as the Founders pray and pour out their innermost heartfelt thoughts seeking divine guidance. I also love how Barbara brings focus by weaving the words from scriptures, quite possibly some of the very words the historical founder themselves may have depended upon for their guidance. How often in the challenges of my own life have I had this same experience and conversations with God—what an incredible and personal gift of insight and reflection. I am truly blessed to count Barbara as a very dear friend, a colleague, and a sister in faith. And I am pleased and honored to enthusiastically recommend this outstanding book to men, women and children alike, of all ages. May it inspire and awaken your desire, creating a hunger to dig deeper and to learn more about our rich history and our incredible God!

Rev. Fred Mast, Pastor, Sedona United Methodist Church

****

It is with great enthusiasm that I offer these words of encouragement for "I Pledge Allegiance to God-What the Founders Write, Say and Pray about God." In this book my friend and sister in Christ, Barbara Schenkel, has offered a glimpse into not only the personal lives of our Founders, but their spiritual lives, as well.

In an engaging and formative manner, Barbara enlightens the reader to another side of history of our nation. She tells the stories of men and women who sought the greater good and worked to create "one nation under God."

Barbara includes a wealth of statements from our Founders that speak to the ongoing efforts in which all citizens are called to be engaged. Samuel Adams in a letter to his wife Betsy, shares, "We must be content to suffer the Loss of all things in this life, rather than tamely surrender the publick liberty...Righteous Heaven will surely smile on a Cause so righteous as ours is, and our Country if it does its Duty will see an end to all Oppressions. Whether I shall live to rejoice with Friends of Liberty and Virtue, my fellow Laborers in the Common Cause, is Matter of no consequence. I will endeavor by God's Assistance to act on my part well, to approve myself to Him and trust everything which concerns me to His all gracious Providence."

Integrity, Honesty, Sacrifice, Humility, Faith.

Barbara's book, "I Pledge Allegiance to God-What the Founders Write, Say and Pray about God", is a reminder of these virtues and their importance to those who built our nation. It is also a reminder to citizens and believers today.

Rev. Neil Leftwich
District Superintendent
Central West District
Desert Southwest Annual Conference
United Methodist Church

Introduction

I have served on the Prayer Team at church for over ten years. In November 2013, I began to put together a special class on the "Prayers of the Clergy, Colonists and Founders" in response to interest shown for this topic from church members and friends.

My interest in the Founders began at our family dinner table when I was growing up. My father loved history, taught history and brought forth many discussions at our evening meals. One summer, after I had finished eighth grade, my father wanted all of us to see something really historic about our country. This meant a two week trip by car to Mount Vernon. We got to see all the rooms of this wonderful house, including the top floor. George and Martha Washington became very real to me. Other places we visited were: Williamsburg, Monticello, Montpelier, Arlington National Cemetery and Washington, D.C.

As I began research on the prayers and God writings of the Founders, I discovered most modern history books, those written in the last 80 years, leave actual God statements of the Founders deleted from their pages. This means one has to search diligently to find the actual God writings of the Founders. Original quotes and prayers of the Founders are what became most important in our class discussions. We talked about *God moments* in the founding of our country and what the Founders felt about God as noted in their writings.

Who is a Founder? Men and women of the generation who lived through the Revolutionary War, the writing of the Declaration of Independence, the adoption of the U.S. Constitution, and who supported the birth of the United States as an independent country. In the wealth of writings the Founders left us, one finds they believed God supported them, not because they were perfect people, but because they believed that liberty to worship God is a God given right.

The result of this research became our first class on "Prayers of the Colonists, Clergy and Founders" which began in January 2014 and a second class in October 2014. I never dreamt this would lead to a book. Through the encouragement of prayer ministry members and class members, *I Pledge Allegiance to God*, has come about.

In discussion with persons inside and outside of the church, I have found great interest in what the Founders wrote and said about God. The focus of this book is on the actual prayers and writings about God of the persons who founded our country, with historical details for background events. Readers will find quotes in their original form, with spelling, capitalization, and use of words somewhat different from today.

This book is written in the present tense to bring the reader into the time and place of each Founder when he or she writes and prays to God. Questions for reflection are included at the end of each chapter.

It is my earnest hope, this book will be a blessing to you and stimulate an interest for you to search further for original writings about God from our nation's Founders. May more *God moments* come your way as you read and share this book with others.

Barbara Schenkel
Phoenix, Arizona
July 2015

Table of Contents

Chapter One

Trust in God

Those who know your name will trust in you, for you, Lord have never forsaken those who seek you. Psalm 9:10

Samuel Adams 1722-1802

Signer of the Declaration of Independence, Signer of the U.S. Constitution, Governor of Massachusetts, Father of the American Revolution

Samuel Adams is born on September 16, 1732 in Boston, Massachusetts. Samuel's family comes directly from the Puritans who came to America for religious freedom. John Cotton, Puritan leader in England, and founding preacher of the first church in Boston, is a relative to Samuel. Samuel learns his ABC's in grade school from the New England Primer which also includes lessons on the Ten Commandments and biblical moral teachings. Samuel and his family attend the Congregational Church. Samuel enters Harvard College in 1736 at age fourteen and graduates in 1740. Samuel tries several jobs such as running a business, but finds his greatest talent is in writing articles and editorial pieces for newspapers.

Samuel throughout his life suffers personal tragedy. His first wife dies after eight years of marriage. Only two of their six children will survive to adulthood. Samuel marries his second wife, Elizabeth Wells on December 6, 1774. Samuel calls her Betsy.

Samuel Is Elected to the Colonial Legislature and Writes Scathing Editorials

Samuel steps up his editorial attacks on the British for taxation without representation, the right to freedom of the press, and the right to freedom of worship. Most significant to Samuel is his trust in God and belief that the laws of God and God's order of nature are the only true basis of government.

Samuel becomes well known for his views and is elected clerk of the local colonial legislature on May 25, 1774. General Thomas Gage, the new British appointed crown governor for Massachusetts Colony, decides the colonists are set against British authority and closes the legislative session down three days later.

General Gage, recognizing Samuel is a thorn in the side of the British, makes one last effort to get Samuel on their side. He sends his aide, Col. Fenton, to offer Samuel a large sum of money. This is described as a "magnificent consideration," if Samuel would cease his hostility to the British Crown Government.

Samuel fires off this reply:

"I trust I have since made my peace with the King of kings. No personal consideration shall induce me to abandon the righteous cause of my country. Tell Governor Gage, it is the advice of Samuel Adams to him, no longer to insult the feelings of an exasperated people."[1]

This results in Samuel being excluded from the general amnesty offered by the British to any citizen of Boston and the Massachusetts Colony who turns in their arms and pleads fealty to King George III. Few colonists take up the offer.

On June 1, 1774, Boston Harbor is shut down by the British in retaliation for 234 chests of tea thrown overboard by the Sons of Liberty the previous December. This causes great hardship for the residents of the town. No longer are they able to receive food, clothing, medicines and other necessities by ship transport.

Samuel, responds passionately on July 25, 1774, in a letter to Andrew Elton Wells:

"Four regiments are encamped upon our Common, while the Harbour is blocked by Ships of War...By such oppressions the British Administration hope to suppress the Spirit of Liberty in this place...The inhabitants are determined to hold out and appeal to the Justice of the Colonies and the World—-trusting God that these things shall be overruled for the Establishment of Liberty, Virtue and Happiness in America."[2]

Samuel and Betsy's Lives Are in Danger

The New Year 1775 brings uneasiness to Samuel and Betsy. British ships of war arrive in Boston with more troops and supplies. Citizens of Boston are arrested and jailed in local British garrisons. Betsy packs essentials as Samuel arranges for both of them to leave their beloved city. In early April, trusted patriot friends come by with a carriage to pick Betsy up. This begins a journey of many months in which Betsy moves from safe house to safe house.

Samuel leaves Boston with John Hancock the second week of April to visit Rev. Jonas Clarke at his parsonage in Lexington. Little do they realize the grave peril this destination put upon their safety. In the early morning hours of April 19, 1775, Paul Revere rushes up on his horse and bangs on Rev. Clarke's front door to roust Samuel and John out of the house. Revere informs them British Regulars have left Boston marching inland with orders to capture Samuel and John. While Samuel and John are considering how to get to Philadelphia where they will meet as elected delegates from Massachusetts to the Second Continental Congress, John Dawes arrives. Dawes tells them British troops are headed to Concord to take over patriot stores of gun powder and rifles. Samuel and John make a hasty escape into the woods. When full morning rises over Lexington, British Regulars and patriot militia are engaged in battle. The Revolutionary War begins as Samuel and John dodge British Regulars on their journey out of Massachusetts Colony. Samuel and John arrive safely in Philadelphia in time for the opening session of Congress on May 5, 1775.

Samuel Agonizes Over His Family's Safety and Prays for the Cause of Liberty

Both Samuel and Betsy worry about family members left in Boston. Samuel's son is imprisoned in a garrison there. So is Betsy's mother and other relatives. The British continue to round up friends and neighbors.

Samuel shares his true feelings with Betsy in writing her these words:

"It is painful for me to be absent from you…If any ill accident has befallen my son or any other person dear to me, I chuse to hear it. Our Boston friends are some of them confined in a Garrison, others dispersed I know not where. Pray, my dear, to let me know as soon as you can."[3]

Betsy writes to Samuel about her fright over hearing the cannon from the Battle of Bunker Hill. Samuel answers back on June 28, 1775 to comfort his wife:

"It is painful for me to reflect upon the Terror I must suppose you were under on hearing the Noise of War so near you…I pray God to cover the heads of our countrymen every day in battle, and ever to protect you from injury in these distracted Times."[4]

Samuel advises Betsy to move to another place other than in the vicinity of Braintree where she has been staying. By the end of summer, Betsy is relocated further away from the war to a house in Dedham.

On October 20, 1775, Samuel believing in the Cause of Liberty states:

"The Affairs of our country are at this moment in the most critical situation. Every Wheel seems now to be in Motion. I am so fully satisfied with the Justice of our Cause, that I can confidently as well as devoutly pray that the righteous Disposer of all things would succeed our Enterprises."[5]

Both Samuel and Betsy do not know when they will be able to return to Boston. Betsy wonders if they will ever return to their home and if it is still in good condition. On November 7, 1775, Samuel writes back to Betsy with this testimony of faith:

"We must be content to suffer the Loss of all things in this life, rather than tamely surrender the publick Liberty…Righteous Heaven will surely smile on a Cause so righteous as ours is, and our Country if it does its Duty will see an end to all Oppressions. Whether I shall live to rejoyce with Friends of Liberty and Virtue, my fellow Laborers in the Common Cause, is Matter of no consequence. I will endeavor by God's Assistance, to act my part well, to approve myself to Him and trust everything which concerns me to His all gracious Providence."[6]

After the adoption of the Declaration of Independence in Congress in July of 1776, Samuel writes a letter to John Adams on September 16, 1776 bearing witness to what it will take to sustain this newly declared liberty:

"May God give us Wisdom, Fortitude, and Perseverance, and every other Virtue necessary for us to maintain that independence which we have asserted."[7]

****

Surely God is my salvation: I will trust and not be afraid. Isaiah 12:2

Abigail Adams 1744-1818

First Lady, Wife of John Adams, Mother of
President John Quincy Adams

Abigail Adams is born on November 11, 1744 in Weymouth, Massachusetts to Rev. William and Elizabeth Smith. Abigail laments that she does not have any formal schooling. She is taught to read and write at home. She receives Bible lessons at home and reads books from her father's library. She especially enjoys reading Shakespeare, Milton and Pope. Her family attends the Congregational Church in Weymouth.

Abigail first meets John Adams in 1759 when she is fourteen years old. John stops by to visit her father when he comes to Weymouth. John and Abigail become friends and eventually marry on October 24, 1764. They move to John's home place in Braintree (now Quincy, Massachusetts). They live in a smaller house built behind the main farm house. They will go on to have four children.

War Comes Close to Home

In June of 1775, Abigail is at the Adams' farm in Braintree alone with the children. John is in Philadelphia attending the Second Continental

Congress. From the top of Penn's Hill behind their house, Abigail can see tall masts of British war ships as they sail into Boston. Abigail hears cannon fire. Messengers come by with the latest news. The Battle of Bunker Hill has begun. Dr. Warren, one of the patriot leaders, is mortally wounded. Abigail takes a few moments out of her busy day to write down a few words of prayer:

"Almighty God cover the heads of our countrymen, and be a shield to our Dear Friends."[8]

Abigail ponders over her list of chores. The vegetable garden needs weeding, the cherry trees need water, dairy cows need milking. Lunch time will be coming soon for the children (all four under the age of twelve years old).

Abigail, knowing the outcome of the Battle of Lexington and Concord on April 19, 1775 and now Bunker Hill, reaffirms in a letter to John on June 18, 1775:

"The race is not to the swift, nor the battle to the strong, but the God of Israel is he that giveth strength and power unto his people. Trust in him at all times, ye people and pour out your hearts before him. God is a refuge for us."[9]

Scores of people pour out of Boston as the battles rage. The road by the Adams' farm becomes clogged with persons who are desperate for a meal or a place to stay. Abigail manages to stay serene while doing what she can to help them. Neighbors and friends stop by every few days to see Abigail to find out if she has heard from John and share the latest news from Boston. Abigail becomes the one person who calms fears, steadies nerves and trusts all things will come out right with God's help.

In the evenings, after the children are in bed, Abigail takes time to pray over the events of the day and reflect on her current situation. She does express her feelings about living in a neighboring town close to Boston and the British Army:

"We live in continual Expectation of Hostilities...but like good Nehemiah having made our prayers to God, set the people with their Swords, their Spears and their bows. We will say unto them, Be not affraid of them. Remember the Lord who is great and terrible, and fight for your brethren, your sons and daughters, your wives and your houses."[10]

The British evacuate Boston on March 17, 1776. The British Navy blows up the lighthouse when they leave. There is a skirmish between patriot defenses and British transports sailing out of the harbor. Abigail can see the tall masts of British ships pulling out.

Abigail composes a prayer for John for his health and strength on June 17, 1776:

"My daily petitions to Heaven for you, are, that you may have Health, Wisdom and fortitude sufficient to carry you thro the great, and arduous Business in which you are engaged; and that your endeavors may be crowned with success."[11]

Through all the daily chores, encounters with anxious travelers on the road by the farm, with sick children, ailing farm animals, broken plows, storms of weather, a war for independence in her midst, Abigail expounds upon her view of it all when she states:

"I feel no great anxiety at the large amount of armyment designed against us. The remarkable interpositions of Heaven in our favor cannot be too gratefully acknowledged. He who fed the Israelites in the wilderness, who clothes the lilies of the Field and feeds the young Ravens when they cry, will not forsake a people engaged in so righteous cause if we remember his Loving kindness."[12]

****

I lift up my eyes to the hills. Where does my help come from? My help comes from the Maker of heaven and earth. Psalm 121:1-2

Benjamin Franklin 1706-1790

Signer of the Declaration of Independence, Diplomat, Scientist, Signer of the U.S. Constitution, Governor of Pennsylvania

Ben Franklin is born in Boston, into a large family of seventeen children on January 17, 1706. His father is a Puritan and brings Ben up learning biblical lessons and moral values. His father hopes Ben will go into the ministry, but has no funds to support this endeavor.

Ben learns rudiments of the printing trade from an older brother. Ben leaves home when he is seventeen years old and travels by boat to New York City. Having little money and finding no work, Ben walks on another ninety-one miles to Philadelphia. He likes his new city and people he meets. He is very tired and hungry when he arrives so he buys bread and drink and eats his lunch. Then he finds a Quaker meeting house, goes in and sits down in the back of the room and sleeps until the Quaker meeting is over.

Ben meets Deborah Reed when he becomes a boarder in her father's house. He finds work as a compositor at a printing establishment. His industry and studious nature become well known.

Ben writes a letter to a friend about his journey to Philadelphia. This friend shows the letter to British Governor Keith of Delaware who offers to set up Ben in a printing shop if he would travel to England to get supplies. Ben sails to London only to find out there is no printing business to set up and Governor Keith has forgotten him. Ben finds work as a journeyman printer. During his time in England, Ben becomes an expert printer and arrives back in Philadelphia in late 1726.

By this time, Deborah Reed is married to Mr. Rogers who runs the family into debt, and leaves Deborah. Sometime later, with narratives around he has another wife, Rogers dies.

By 1730, Ben has set himself up as a respectable printer in Philadelphia and begins courting Deborah. They marry on September 1. Deborah has much common sense, some business acumen, and assists Ben in running the shop. Deborah and Ben will have two children. One dies in infancy and their daughter Sarah, grows to adulthood. Ben already has one son, William, who they raise as their own.

Ben as a young man has met scrupulous and unscrupulous people, met educated and uneducated people. He decides on certain values as being most important to him. These are: to be thrifty, to speak the truth, to be hardworking, to speak ill of no one, and to help others in need.

Ben's Skepticism Regarding Church Dogma

Ben comments he has had a difficult time with established church dogma. He discusses religious belief by stating:

"I never was without some religious principles; I never doubted, for instance, the existence of a Deity; that he made the world, and governed it by his providence; that the acceptable service to God was the doing of good to man; that our souls are immortal, and virtue is rewarded either here or in the hereafter."[13]

Ben states he was educated as a Presbyterian, but found some of the church dogmas unintelligible. Rarely did he find a preacher he liked who would emphasize morality, rather than church teachings.

One exception is Rev. Whitfield who is an Anglican evangelist who comes to the colonies to preach in 1739. As a student earlier in his life, Whitfield studies at Oxford and while there becomes a member of the Holy Club with John and Charles Wesley. Holy Club members get up every morning at 4 a.m. to pray several hours before breakfast.

Ben and Rev. Whitfield Become Good Friends

Whitfield is an itinerant preacher who preaches mostly out of doors in the fields and out in the streets of towns. In Philadelphia over five thousand persons come to hear Rev. Whitfield one evening. Persons from every sect and religious background crowd the streets. Ben exclaims:

"It is wonderful to see the change soon made in the manners of the inhabitants. From being thoughtless and indifferent to religion, it seemed as if all the world were growing religious, so that one could not walk through the town in the evening without hearing psalms sung in different families of every street."[14]

Ben buys a pew at Christ Church (Anglican) in Philadelphia. Deborah and Sarah attend church there and are communicants. Ben gladly prints Rev. Whitfield's sermons for many years. Ben continues to publish his own almanac, *Poor Richard's Almanac*, which is very popular with the general public.

In 1765, the British pass the Stamp Act which requires the purchase of officially stamped paper for use to print any public documents in the colonies. This includes newspapers, deeds, books, bills of lading, and court documents. Colonists turn out in the streets to protest.

Just before the Stamp Act is passed, Rev. Whitfield returns to England to raise money for an orphanage he founds in the colony of Georgia. Ben corresponds with Whitfield and sails to England in 1765 to address the

British Parliament. Rev. Whitfield goes with Ben to the British lawmakers and both implore parliament to repeal the Stamp Act. The Stamp Act is repealed shortly thereafter.

Ben Begins His Career with the Continental Congress

In 1775, Ben is appointed Postmaster General for the colonies by the Continental Congress. In addition, he serves as a member of the Pennsylvania Committee of Safety. Ben is elected as a delegate representing Pennsylvania to the Continental Congress and signs the Declaration of Independence in 1776. Later the same year, Ben begins his diplomatic career in Paris, France. He is able to negotiate an alliance for arms and supplies for the Continental Army. Ben continues as America's diplomat in France throughout the Revolutionary War and is part of the negotiating team who signs a peace treaty with Great Britain in 1783.

Ben Attends the Constitutional Convention

In 1787, Ben becomes a delegate representing Pennsylvania at the Constitutional Convention in Philadelphia. During the months of May to late June, the various delegates could not arrive at an agreement on setting up the new government. On June 28, 1787, Ben stands up and addresses the convention:

"Mr. President, the small progress we have made after four or five weeks close attendance and continual reasonings with each other...in this situation of this Assembly, groping as it were in the dark to find political truth and scarce able to distinguish it when presented to us, how has it happened, Sir, that we have not hither to once thought of humbly applying to the Father of lights, to illuminate our understanding? In the beginning of the contest with Great Britain, when we were sensible of danger, we had daily prayer in this room for divine protection. Our prayers, Sir, were heard, and they were graciously answered. All of us who engaged in the struggle must have observed frequent instances of superintending Providence in our favor. To that kind Providence we own this happy opportunity of consulting in peace on the means of establishing our future felicity. And now we have forgotten that powerful Friend?...We have been assured, Sir, in the Sacred Writings, that *except the Lord built the house, they labour in vain that built it.* I firmly believe this...I therefore beg leave to move that henceforth prayers, imploring the assistance of Heaven and its blessings on our deliberations, be held in this assembly every morning before we proceed to business."[15]

In a *God moment,* the delegates adjourn for three days. One of their first actions is to attend church in Philadelphia and pray together. On July 2, 1787, when the Constitutional Convention meets again, delegates work in harmony and adopt the new U.S. Constitution.

****

I am the vine; you are the branches. If any man remains in me and I in him, he will bear much fruit; apart from me you can do nothing. John 15:5

Dr. Benjamin Rush 1745-1813

Signer of the Declaration of Independence, Surgeon General of the Continental Army, Father of American Medicine, Founder of Five Colleges, Founder of the First Sunday School in Pennsylvania, and Founder with Benjamin Franklin of the first Abolition Society in Pennsylvania

Benjamin Rush is born in Byberry, Pennsylvania fourteen miles northeast (now a thriving suburb) of Philadelphia December 24, 1745. When Benjamin is six years old, his father dies leaving his mother to raise Benjamin and his siblings alone. His mother moves her children to Philadelphia and runs a grocery store in the city to make a living for her family.

Benjamin, being a studious youth, leaves home at age nine to enter an academy in Maryland. He completes his preparatory studies and goes on to Princeton College, graduating in 1760 at the age of fifteen.

After this, Benjamin takes up the study of medicine in Philadelphia. He further studies in England, France and Scotland where he graduates with a Doctor of Medicine degree from Edinburgh.

Dr. Rush Begins His Medical Practice

In 1763, Benjamin, not only has a private practice in Philadelphia, but also begins his teaching career at the College of Philadelphia where he becomes widely known throughout the colonies as Dr. Rush.

In 1774, Dr. Rush becomes well known for his views on liberty, abolition and for his believing in Jesus Christ. That same year, Dr. Rush and Benjamin Franklin found the Abolition Society of Philadelphia.

Dr. Rush Is a Delegate to the Continental Congress

The year 1776 is a momentous one. In January, Dr. Rush marries Judith Stockton. They will go on to have thirteen children. In June, he receives appointment as a member of the Pennsylvania Provincial Congress and begins to draft a resolution recommending independence. In July, Dr.

Rush is elected as a delegate to the Continental Congress and signs the Declaration of Independence.

In December, Dr. Rush travels as a civilian doctor to the army with Pennsylvania troops under General Cadawalader in the Battle of Trenton and Battle of Princeton. Dr. Rush treats wounded soldiers in hospital encampments. Dr. Rush returns to Baltimore the end of January 1777 to serve again in the Continental Congress.

Dr. Rush meets his good friend, John Adams, at the Congress. Dr. Rush asks about the success of the war. John Adams replies:

"We shall succeed in our struggle, provided we repent of our sins and forsake them."[16]

Dr. Rush is Appointed Surgeon General

In April 1777, Dr. Rush is appointed Surgeon General for the Continental Army, Middle Department. Dr. Rush begins to grapple with the lack of medical supplies, medicines, and keeping hospital areas clean. He serves in this capacity until January 1778. Dr. Rush, after leaving the post of Surgeon General, writes a medical book describing medical techniques for treating wounded soldiers. His book is entitled, *Directions for Preserving the Health of Soldiers*. This book becomes a standard medical reference used through the Civil War.

Dr. Rush Returns to His Medical Practice

By 1770, Dr. Rush has become a professor at the now University of the State of Pennsylvania and goes on to write many medical articles and instructs over 3,000 medical students.

Through all the years of his medical practice, Dr. Rush focuses on the poor and God's help stating:

"To his goodness in accepting my services to poor children, I ascribe the innumerable blessings of my life...It is not to him that willeth, nor him that runneth, but to the overruling hand of Heaven that we are to look for the successful issue of all human events."[17]

Dr. Rush Founds the First Sunday School in Philadelphia

Dr. Rush founds a Sunday School program to teach children to read the Bible. He writes:

"Useful education in a republic is to be laid in religion...Without this there can be no virtue, and without virtue there can be no liberty...By religion I mean...to recommend the New Testament...a Christian cannot fail of being useful to the republic, for his religion teaches him that no man liveth to himself."[18]

Dr. Rush is very concerned about how children develop virtue and morals. He passionately states:

"Mothers and schoolmasters plant the seeds of nearly all the good and evil which exists in the world."[19]

Dr. Rush Supports the Abolition Society

Dr. Rush's other great commitment is to the Abolition Society of Philadelphia. He notes that:

"The history of creation of man, and the relation of our species to each other by birth, which is recorded in the Old Testament, is the best refutation that can be given to the divine right of kings and the strongest argument that can be used in favor of the original and natural equality of mankind."[20]

Dr. Rush helps the Abolition Society and donates five thousand acres of land so that fifty acre plots of land are deeded over to black families to live on. Dr. Rush supports the founding of several black churches in Philadelphia and lobbies to pass laws to end slavery in Pennsylvania.

Yellow Fever Epidemic Hits Philadelphia

August 1793 brings a Yellow Fever epidemic to Philadelphia. The epidemic strikes fiercely and without warning. Thousands of citizens and visitors become ill. Many more people flee the city out of fear. Dr. Rush and other physicians set up hospital wards. At one point, there are only three physicians, including Dr. Rush, to treat about forty thousand patients.

At this time, Philadelphia is the nation's capital. President Washington and Martha leave the city as Martha is concerned for their health and persuades George to leave. The government and many businesses shut down. Dr. Rush comes down with Yellow Fever twice and survives.

Whether Dr. Rush is founding a school for women in Philadelphia, founding a Sunday School for children, training doctors, reforming alcoholics, supporting the Abolition Society, or assisting to found the Bible Society of Philadelphia, he would say all was done for his Savior, Jesus Christ.

****

Chapter One Questions for Reflection

1. How does Samuel Adams say he can confidently rely on the outcome of justice of our cause to succeed? What does Samuel Adams

ask God for so Americans can maintain their independence after signing the Declaration of Independence?

2. What does Abigail Adams say is the responsibility of a people engaged in so righteous a cause? What remarkable interpositions of Heaven in our favor is Abigail Adams writing about?
3. What four values does Benjamin Franklin say are the most important to a person's life? During the Constitutional Convention, what does Benjamin Franklin say the delegates need to do the first thing before beginning their meeting each day?
4. Who does Dr. Rush say are the two most important persons in a child's life to promote public and private order in society? Do you agree with Dr. Rush that a free government or free society not founded on teachings of the Bible must perish? Why or why not? See Psalm 119:45-48, and 2 Corinthians 3:17.

Chapter Two

Hope in God

We have this hope as an anchor for the soul, firm and secure. Hebrews 6:19a

Nathanael Greene 1742-1786

Major General of the Continental Army

Nathanael Greene is born in Warwick, Rhode Island on August 7, 1742 into a Quaker family. He is one of six children, all boys. His father is a Quaker leader who encourages his sons to learn the Bible. The elder Greene runs a mill and iron forge on the Potowomut Peninsula. The forge makes large anchors for ships and other fishing gear. The Greene Mill grinds grain brought by the local farmers and ships out the grain to other parts of the colonies. Nathanael's mother dies when he is eleven years old.

By 1770, when his father dies, Nathanael is living at the family forge business in Coventry. Coventry is a small village with few amenities so Nathanael spends his time reading books, and adding to his personal library that grows to over two hundred fifty volumes. Nathanael learns about the history of other governments such as the Romans and Greeks. He studies the laws and culture of medieval Europe. Most important to him are Blackstone's commentary on the laws of Great Britain and John Locke's Civil Government essays.

Nathanael's Concern for Rhode Island Grows

In 1774, Nathanael agrees to serve on Rhode Island's Committee of Safety. He assists to revise Rhode Island's militia laws. Also that year, on July 20, Nathanael marries Catherine Littlefield at her aunt's house in Greenwich.

Nathanael knows Boston well having gone there to conduct business for the family forge and mills. One of his favorite book stores in Boston is run by Henry Knox. In a few months these two friends will end up serving together in the Continental Army. When the British blockade the port of Boston, Nathanael is outraged.

Nathanael and fifty-four other Rhode Islanders are alarmed about the safety of the Rhode Island Colony. Providence, their main city, is only fifty miles from Boston. In October 1774, the Rhode Island Assembly officially authorizes the militia. Nathanael becomes a private in the militia and attends drill sessions three times a week.

When the British attack Lexington and Concord on April 19, 1775, the Rhode Island General Assembly meets in an emergency meeting and forms the Rhode Island militia of fifteen hundred men.

Nathanael Is Appointed General of the Rhode Island Militia

In a moment that becomes a *God Moment,* the Rhode Island General Assembly pass over all the veteran candidates with battlefield experience, and appoint Nathanael Greene as the General of the Rhode Island Regiment. No one in Rhode Island that day realizes they have just appointed a leader who would become one of history's most successful generals in the Continental Army. Nathanael throughout his life would be the one person who made military decisions without regard for personal glory, with concern for his troops, and with a true heart for the completion of the mission at hand. What Nathanael demonstrates to his contemporaries is his ability to lead troops. With his positive personality, a hope in God for the future, and an outright commitment to the task at hand, Nathanael is able to step into a leadership role.

After this announcement, Nathanael explains to his wife Kitty about his appointment:

"I have no doubt I shall be conducted safely through Tory hail...We are all in the hands of the great Jehovah; to him let us look for protection...Let us then put our confidence in God, and recommend our souls to his care."[21]

General Greene becomes known for his organization of the Rhode Island Regiment. Camp is to be clean and neat, soldiers themselves to be clean, uniforms, equipment and rifles are to be clean, and the camp latrines reburied each day. As a result, Rhode Islanders suffer less illness than other regiments in the army.

Nathanael Becomes General Washington's Confidant

General Washington comes out to inspect the various regiments after he is appointed Commander of the Continental Army. Upon inspecting the well-organized Rhode Island camp, Washington appoints Nathanael a Brigadier General in the Continental Army. Nathanael goes on to become General Washington's right hand man and confidant in the running of army business and affairs. Nathanael believes so much in Washington's skills and abilities, he always has a word of hope for his commanding general. Washington sends Nathanael to speak to the Continental Congress about pressing army affairs when he personally cannot leave his post as Commander of the Army. Washington knows he can trust Nathanael to be true to his word.

After the Battle of Princeton, Nathanael describes what happened:

"Divine Providence has given a very favorable turn to affairs, and at an hour when people least expected it…He that goes to war and always expects a flowing tide is a novice at heart and ignorant of human affairs… Nay, I think we have abundant cause to bless God that our sufferings have not been greater than we have."[22]

General Greene continues in his duties as quarter master and joins General Washington in command of troops as needed.

Benedict Arnold Becomes a Traitor

One night late on September 25, 1780, a messenger comes into Nathanael's camp (at Orangewood, New York), and hands him a letter from Colonel Alexander Hamilton. The letter informs Nathanael of Benedict Arnold's actions to hand West Point military post over to the British. Nathanael immediately sends troops to West Point to insure the British do not capture the post. Nathanael and his aides do not sleep until they are informed the Continental Army has secured West Point.

Nathanael pens a note to his wife Kitty about Arnold:

"The discovery appears to have been Providential and convinces me that the liberties of America are the object of divine protection. God grant that all such perfidy come to light and the torn meet with their just desert."[23]

Nathanael Greene is promoted to Commander of the Southern Department of the Continental Army and wins the war against the British in South Carolina. Writing about his Rhode Island troops, Nathanael proudly proclaims:

"God Almighty inclined their hearts...and they engaged anew. This is the greatest example of N.E. (New England) virtue that I ever saw."[24]

****

We wait in hope for the Lord; he is our help and shield. Psalm 33:20

Thomas Jefferson 1743-1826

Author and Signer of the Declaration of Independence, Diplomat, Governor of Virginia, Third President of the United States

Thomas Jefferson's business manager, Captain Edmund Bacon, whom Thomas hires as the overseer of the Monticello estate, describes about Jefferson:

"He had a large Bible, which nearly always lay at the head of his sofa. Many and many a time I have gone into his room and found him reading the Bible...Some people, you know, say he was an atheist. Now if he was an atheist, what did he want with all those religious books, and why did he spend so much of his time reading the Bible?"[25]

Thomas Jefferson is born at his parents' home in Albemarle County, Virginia on April 13, 1743. Thomas attends grammar school at age five then goes on to private school at age nine to study classics. At age sixteen, Thomas enters William and Mary College and graduates two years later. He then studies law with George Wythe and is admitted to the bar in 1767.

Thomas already is a landowner. At age fourteen he inherits two thousand acres of plantation land and thirty slaves when his father dies. Thomas attends the Anglican Church growing up and as an adult serves as a vestryman.

Thomas marries Martha Wayles Skelton on January 1, 1772. Thomas is blessed with a happy marriage and six children. Generous at heart, Thomas takes in his sister and her six children when her husband Dabney Carr dies. Thomas raises her children as his own. Only two of Thomas' natural children survive to adulthood.

Thomas Is an Elected Member of the House of Burgesses

Being a member of the Virginia House of Burgesses, Thomas is able to support a bill which abolishes slavery in Virginia. George Washington also supports this bill to get it passed.

Irate that the Virginia local government passes such a bill against slavery and British policy, the British Crown appointed governor, vetoes the bill.

In 1773, Thomas joins the Virginia Committee of Correspondence. Each of the 13 colonies has such a committee to keep in touch with one another about the latest news regarding British laws in the colonies, movements of British troops, and British treatment of colonists.

Thomas writes a pamphlet entitled, "The Summary View of the Rights of British America."

This pamphlet upsets Governor Lord Dunmore who threatens to arrest Thomas for high treason. The House of Burgesses backs up Thomas. Governor Lord Dunmore does not arrest Thomas, but does dismiss the House of Burgesses. In 1775, Thomas is elected as a delegate from Virginia to the Continental Congress.

The Colonies Declare Independence from Great Britain

In June of 1776, a committee is appointed by Congress to review the Virginia Resolutions, the Mecklenburg Resolutions and other statements for separation of the thirteen colonies from Great Britain. Thomas Jefferson, Roger Sherman, Ben Franklin, Robert Livingston, and John Adams become members of the committee. On June 11, 1776, John Adams tells Thomas to become the head of the committee and to write a draft of a declaration for independence from Great Britain. Thomas turns in his first draft on June 28 to the committee. In his first draft Thomas writes these words:

"We hold these truths to be sacred and undeniable that all men are created equal and independent; that from that equal creation they deserve rights inherent and unalienable, among which are the preservation of life, and liberty, and the pursuit of happiness."[26]

The committee reviews Thomas's draft. Ben Franklin and John Adams make changes to some words and inform Thomas to take out all references to King George III causing slavery in the colonies. Congress wants the final draft by July 2.

Thomas goes to his room and spends the next four days writing a new draft. In a dramatic *God moment,* Thomas writes the final draft of the Declaration of Independence to present to Congress on July 2, 1776:

"We hold these truths to be self-evident: that all men are created equal; that they are endowed by their Creator with certain unalienable rights; among these are life, liberty, and the pursuit of happiness."[27]

Congress adopts the Declaration of Independence and the world's concept of self-government is changed.

Thomas returns home when his wife Martha becomes ill. Thomas resigns from Congress and is elected to serve in the Virginia Assembly instead. Thomas along with Ben Franklin and Silas Deane are appointed to a committee to negotiate alliances with France. Thomas declines the journey to France as he must stay home with Martha. Thomas is elected Governor of Virginia and serves in that capacity from 1779-1781.

Thomas' world falls apart when his wife Martha dies in 1782. Thomas rarely attends his home Anglican Church after this. Thomas buries himself in his work, and eventually travels to France in 1784 to join the American delegation in their negotiations for a peace treaty with Great Britain.

Thomas Becomes the Third President of the United States

Thomas' crowning achievement through all the offices he held for his country is to be elected the third President of the United States. Thomas ends his first inaugural address with this prayer:

"And may the Infinite Power which rules the destinies of the universe lead our councils to what is best, and give them a favorable issue for your peace and prosperity."[28]

As president, Thomas attends church service every Sunday at the Capitol building when he is in Washington, D.C. He sits in the same seat on the front row and enjoys sermons from clergymen of all denominations. Thomas gives donations to eight separate churches while he is president.

It is during Thomas Jefferson's presidency, that Napoleon sells to the United States the city of New Orleans, and the Louisiana Territory for fifteen million dollars. The United States acquires over eight hundred thousand acres and access to the mouth of the Mississippi River. Thomas acts wisely and expediently in completing this sale.

****

May our Lord Jesus Christ himself and God our Father, who loved us and by his grace gave us eternal encouragement and good hope, encourage your hearts and strengthen you in every good deed and word. 2 Thessalonians 2:16-17.

Rev. John Witherspoon 1723-1794

Signer of the Declaration of Independence, President of the College of New Jersey (now Princeton University), Presbyterian Minister of the Gospel

John Witherspoon is born in Edinburgh, Scotland in 1723 to a Presbyterian minister and his family. His mother's family are direct descendants of John Knox who started the Protestant movement in Scotland. By age four, John is able to read the Bible. John enters the University of Edinburgh at age thirteen, earning a Master of Arts degree at age sixteen and a Master of Divinity degree at age twenty.

John becomes an ordained Presbyterian minister when he is twenty-two years old and begins serving his first church in Beith, Scotland. John marries Elizabeth Montgomery when he is twenty-five years old. They will go on to have ten children; five of which live into adulthood.

In 1757, John moves to Paisley and becomes well known for his sermons with over one thousand persons coming to hear him preach on Sunday mornings. John is known for teaching:

"A foolish and unreasonable supposition is that a man can believe wrongly, and yet live a good life."[29]

Rev. Witherspoon Moves to America

In 1766, College of New Jersey staff start looking for a new college president to direct their school. The new leader has to be one of strength, impeccable reputation, and a gospel preacher who would uphold personal commitment to Christ and evangelism as priorities. The College of New Jersey located at Princeton becomes well known for training Presbyterian ministers for the church. An offer is made to Rev. Witherspoon to come to America to lead the school.

Benjamin Rush, happens to be a medical student in Edinburgh at the time. He agrees to visit Rev. Witherspoon in Paisley. Other letters of support arrive from America asking John and his family to come to New Jersey. In August of 1768, Rev. Witherspoon and his family arrive in Princeton to settle in. John officially becomes the new President of the College of New Jersey on August 17. To welcome their new president, at evening, students place lit candles in each window of Nassau Hall, the main classroom and dorm building on campus.

Rev. Witherspoon expands the classes at the college to include science, more Latin and Greek, mathematics, moral and natural philosophy and also teaches theology classes for the ministers in training, emphasizing to all,

"Godliness with contentment is great gain."[30]

Science classes are held in the family's large garden at their two story stone farm house a mile from the college.

Rev. Witherspoon Joins the Cause of Liberty

By July of 1774, New Jersey begins a Committee of Correspondence. Committee members keep in touch with each other throughout the colonies on British taxation issues, trade and treatment of colonists. Rev. Witherspoon supports the rights of the colonists. Being from Scotland he knows first-hand of the hardship the British could place upon their subjects.

Rev. Witherspoon meets with seventy-two other men in New Jersey to draw up resolutions against the British and elect five delegates to the Continental Congress. Rev. Witherspoon serves first on the New Jersey state Constitutional Convention. When issues get tough,

Rev. Witherspoon tells his fellow delegates,

"God is the author of every blessing."[31]

On June 22, 1776, Rev. Witherspoon accepts election to represent New Jersey at the Continental Congress and signs the Declaration of Independence when it is passed by Congress.

Rev. Witherspoon becomes a member of the committee to procure wagons and uniforms for the Continental Army. He sets up a Scottish weaver in Nassau Hall at the College of New Jersey to make uniforms. Later on Rev. Witherspoon becomes a member of the Foreign Affairs Committee.

In November 1776, Rev. Witherspoon rides back to Princeton to dismiss students at the college due to the war being fought in New Jersey. By the end of December, Elizabeth and one daughter, Frances, pack up as many belongings as they can get into a carriage. They leave in the carriage with Rev. Witherspoon on horseback to head to Pennsylvania. Sons John Jr. and James are serving in the Continental Army. Another son, David is in Virginia visiting friends.

The British capture Princeton and raid the college. British troops tear apart Rev. Witherspoon's library and office. Many of his papers, sermons, and books are destroyed in a fire set in the library. Nassau Hall is used by the British troops as a barracks for the three weeks they are there. In a battle with the Continental Army in January 1777, the British destroy parts of Nassau Hall including the Prayer Chapel and organ. The Witherspoon stone farm house is left intact. The livestock are run off and gardens torn up.

In one of his sermons, Rev. Witherspoon extols his congregation with these words:

"You are all my witnesses, that this is the first time of my introducing my political subject into the pulpit. At this session, however, it is not only lawful but necessary, and I willingly embrace the opportunity of declaring my opinion without any hesitation, that the cause in which America is now in arms, is the cause of justice, of liberty...The knowledge of God and his truths has been chiefly confined to those parts of the earth where some degree of liberty and political justice were to be seen."[32]

Rev. Witherspoon's Influence Reaches into the Next Generation

Rev. Witherspoon is able to reopen the College of New Jersey for classes on July 10, 1777. Nassau Hall is being used as a hospital for Continental troops. Parts of the building are without windows or adequate repairs so students stay with families in the community. Rev. Witherspoon continues to build up the College of New Jersey and establishes this school as more than a seminary for ministers. The College of New Jersey eventually becomes Princeton University.

Rev. Witherspoon has influence into the future through his students. James Madison studies theology and ethics in graduate courses with Rev. Witherspoon. Ministers graduate and take Rev. Witherspoon's teaching out into their churches.

In 1794, Rev. Witherspoon becomes moderator for the first General Assembly of the Presbyterian Church in the United States. He is able to draw various Presbyterian groups into a united church.

****

Lord, you establish peace for us, all that we have accomplished you have done for us. Isaiah 26:12

Richard Bassett 1745-1815

Captain of Delaware militia in the Revolutionary War, Signer of the U.S. Constitution, U.S. Senator, Presidential Elector who voted for John Adams, Governor of Delaware, Methodist lay preacher.

Richard is born April 2, 1745 in Cecil County, Maryland to a tavern keeper. His father abandons the family when Richard is very young. Richard grows up relying on his maternal relations for assistance. Richard becomes a lawyer with the assistance of Mr. Lawson, a relative, who becomes Richard's mentor. When Lawson dies, Richard inherits a six thousand acre estate known as Bohemia Manor near the Maryland-Delaware boundary line. Richard marries Ann Ennals; she dies leaving no children. Richard then marries Miss Bruff from Talbot County; they have one daughter.

In 1770, Richard receives a license to practice law in Dover, Delaware. He becomes well known for his hospitality and charity work. In 1774, Richard is elected to serve on the Boston Relief Committee for Delaware. Richard becomes part of patriotic efforts against the British. Richard serves on a committee that drafts Delaware's constitution.

Richard Joins the Delaware Militia

In 1776, Richard becomes a captain in the Dover militia. Richard organizes Haslett's Regiment, the only regiment of Continental Regulars recruited in Delaware. Richard goes on to organize a mobile reserve militia with ten-thousand recruits known as Flying Camp, that provides General Washington troops during the war. Richard volunteers in 1777 to join General Rodney's unit to patrol a corridor to keep the British Army out of Philadelphia and protect Baltimore from British forces. After the British withdraw from Delaware, Richard continues as commander of the Dover Light Horse, Kent County's militia unit.

Richard Represents Delaware at the Constitutional Convention

In 1786, Richard is elected to represent Delaware at the Annapolis Convention. This is a meeting called by James Madison and Alexander Hamilton to plan for trade agreements among the colonies. In 1787, Richard is elected to represent Delaware at the Constitutional Convention in Philadelphia. Richard represents Delaware very wisely, always aware of protecting Delaware's interests as a small state against larger states. Richard attends every session and speaks on state's rights. He does realize a need for a national government to promote economic trade and regulate foreign affairs. Due to Richard's efforts, Delaware becomes the first state to adopt the U.S. Constitution.

Richard Is Elected a U.S. Senator from Delaware

In 1789, Richard is elected a U.S. Senator from Delaware. As a senator, Richard supports President Washington's right to control the executive branch and develop the power of the Presidency. Richard allies himself with the Federalist Party and supports Vice-President John Adams.

In agreeing with sentiments in Delaware, Richard becomes the first to vote for locating the national capital away from either New York or Philadelphia. Richard feels strong about this issue.

In 1793, Richard is elected as Chief Justice of the Court of Common Pleas in Delaware, and ends his term in the Senate. In 1796, Richard is chosen as an elector for the Electoral College and votes to elect John Adams president. In 1799, Richard is elected Governor of Delaware.

Richard Becomes a Methodist Lay Preacher

Richard is known as one of the most devout of the founders. Earlier in his life, Richard meets Bishop Francis Asbury, the first Bishop of the Methodist Episcopal Church in America. Richard, who grew up in the Anglican Church, finds his heart warmed in faith in his meeting with Bishop Asbury. Richard joins the Methodist movement in 1779 and becomes a lay preacher. Richard teaches faith in Christ to persons who come to meetings held at his home. He works diligently to found one of the first Methodist Churches in the Dover area in 1784. Richard preaches at Methodist Society meetings.

In one of his sermons, Richard attacks skeptics who refuse to believe in anything they can not see or touch. Richard exhorts he does not understand:

"How a man could believe by this rule that he had a back, as he could not see it unless he had a neck like a crane or a goose."[33]

Bishop Asbury writes in his journal April 27, 1780, about Richard:

"A very conversant and affectionate man, who, from his own acknowledgements, appears to be sick of sin."[34]

Richard repents of his sins and frees all of his slaves. Richard and his wife become supporters of the Methodist circuit riders in the area by giving them room and board when they are in town.

****

Be joyful in hope, patient in affliction, faithful in prayer. Romans 12:12

Martha Washington 1731-1802

First Lady of the Land, wife of President George Washington

Martha is born on June 2, 1731 at Chestnut Grove Plantation in New Kent County, Virginia. She is the oldest daughter of John Dandridge. Chestnut Grove has a new house with six large rooms. John Dandridge is very proud of his life in the Virginia Colony. He arrives in 1715 when he is fifteen years old with an older brother. John works diligently as a deputy clerk of the court and within seven years he is able to buy Chestnut Grove in 1730. That same year, John marries Frances Jones and becomes a county clerk and serves in the New Kent militia.

Martha grows up with three younger brothers and four younger sisters. Martha learns early to take care of her younger sibs and many other domestic duties. Martha attends St. Peter's Anglican Church every Sunday with her family. Her father is a vestryman. Martha and her family read the Bible, the Anglican Book of Prayer, and take communion at church.

Martha marries Daniel Parke Custis on May 15, 1750. They have four children: Daniel Parke Custis who dies when he is two years old, Frances Parke Custis who dies when she is four years old, John Park Custis and Martha Parke Custis. This leaves Martha with two children, John who is called Jacky and Martha who is called Patsy, when her first husband Daniel dies at age forty-five on July 8, 1757.

Martha Is Left to Run the Custis Estate

Martha is left alone to run all of Daniel Custis' estates. Martha shows much determination and spunk in dealing with debts Daniel owes, paying taxes, selling tobacco crops to agents in England, and ongoing record keeping. Martha and her children inherit farms and 250 slaves. Daniel Custis set up in his will that his slaves could not be sold; rather they would stay in the Custis family from generation to generation.

Several older gentlemen begin courting Martha. Martha does not make any commitment to them, knowing she would be well off. She is more concerned for her children's well-being.

Martha Marries George Washington

In March of 1758, Martha is visiting friends at Richard Chamberlayne's home at Poplar Grove and meets a young Colonel Washington, from the Virginia militia, who has stopped by on his way to Williamsburg. Visitors at the Chamberlayne's notice George and Martha stay up visiting late into the night. George later calls on Martha at her home. A few months later they become engaged. George and Martha marry on January 6, 1759 at Martha's home. Rev. David Mossom of St. Peter's Anglican Church officiates. George and Martha stay in New Kent County for a month. Then Martha moves in with George at Mount Vernon. Along with Martha are her two children, Patsy who is four years old and Jacky who is five years old.

Martha spends an hour in the morning each day upstairs in a sitting area by her desk, reading the Bible and praying with the Anglican Book of Prayer. Servants are instructed not to interrupt her.

Martha is known for her outgoing personality and positive attitude in tough times. Visitors to Mount Vernon comment on her upbeat spirit. Edward Pendleton on a visit to Mount Vernon comments on what Martha states to him after the war has started,

"I hope you will stand firm—-I know George will."[35]

When Pendleton, Patrick Henry and George leave to go to Philadelphia, Martha tells them,

"God be with you, gentlemen."[36]

Martha Travels to Continental Army Camps

Once the war begins George is away at Continental Army camps. Martha is not one to stay away from camp for long. With a boundless spirit of boldness, Martha plans well ahead for her trips to the Continental Army camp. Several days before departure, Martha collects blankets, sewing materials to make shirts for the soldiers, knitting supplies and wool to make socks for the soldiers, medicinal supplies including brandy, bandages, and other home remedies. The day before leaving, wagons are loaded up with these supplies plus smoked Virginia hams, smoked bacon, smoked beef, dried fruit, onions, molasses and cornmeal.

Martha usually leaves home in cold weather when there is ice and snow on the roads. Bundled up as best as she can be in her carriage, Martha is accompanied by a Virginia Regiment of Continentals who become known as Lady Washington's Brigade. George sees to it that she has reliable teams of horses to draw her carriage. One year George buys her a matched pair of bay horses for the task.

Martha's normal schedule is a five day trip just to Philadelphia through rutted roads and windy snow blown into drifts. Martha stays several days in the city to recover from the jarring rides in the coach.

Martha Is Welcomed in Philadelphia

Martha meets many dignitaries who come to see her since she is General Washington's wife. Martha greets them all with her smile and gracious compliments. Whether she intends to be or not, Martha becomes George's goodwill ambassador. Martha is able to soothe hurt feelings, calm anxious persons, lift up dour outlooks from members of the Continental Congress, and speak to Philadelphia's wealthy supporters of the Continental Army.

On one occasion in Philadelphia, some of the wealthy society families plan to give Martha a party to celebrate her arrival. This would include dancing, serving wine and other libations with much fanfare and opulence. More staid members of the community, including Patriots and Quakers, are concerned the partying would give a negative message to the community; the common person on the street, and the suffering soldiers in the field. Philadelphia society members are in an uproar. Not wanting to offend Lady Washington or their neighbors, the situation becomes delicate for many citizens. Patriot committee members call on Martha and explain their circumstances. Martha tactfully declines to attend the party which then is cancelled.

Martha Arrives at Her First Winter Encampment

Martha's first trip to winter encampment begins on November 21, 1775 when she leaves Mount Vernon to arrive December 11, after traveling five hundred miles, in Cambridge, Massachusetts. When she arrives in Cambridge, Martha observes that Christ Church, the Anglican Church in town is closed. Martha informs George the church needs to be opened for services. Martha takes on the task of getting the building ready. The church is cleaned up inside after having been used as a barracks for the soldiers.

Colonel Palfrey of Boston is the church service leader. When all have been seated in a pew, people gather to sing psalms and Palfrey gives the message. Dorothy Dudley takes down notes in her journal about the service and General Washington, January 1, 1776:

"Yesterday service was held at Christ Church. Col. Palfrey read the service and made a prayer of the form different from that commonly used for the king...The General's majestic figure bent reverently in prayer as with devout earnestness he entered into the service."[37] Before the Anglican Church was reopened, Martha and George attend Rev. Appleton's Congregational Church in Cambridge.

A few days later, expecting Lady Washington to be dressed in silks, brocades, and wearing fancy jewelry, Quaker wives call on Martha. Instead, they find a plainly dressed Martha who is able to converse with them in a way that puts these farm wives at ease. Martha listens to their concerns about their families and the war. The Quaker wives find Lady Washington is very down to earth as she gladly wishes God's blessings upon them.

Martha Cares for the Sick and Wounded

Martha appoints herself to care for the sick and wounded soldiers in camp. She walks daily to visit the sickest, and the most severely wounded soldiers in the camp hospital or in their huts. Martha brings a delicacy of food, or a blanket, or stockings or a shirt to the soldiers. On one visit with a soldier, Martha:

"knelt down by his straw pallet and prayed earnestly for him and his wife in her sweet and solemn voice."[38]

Martha confidently exhibits fortitude and hope. Martha is known for saying,

"God knows where we shall be."[39]

Martha Manages Officers' Wives Social Events

At General Washington's headquarters, Martha takes over activities for the other officers' wives. Together they sew shirts and knit socks for the soldiers, and plan social activities for the evenings. Martha is able to chart a peaceable course through the varying personalities of the wives of the other officers. Martha is sure to address each one's concerns for their husbands and their children and ensure a place for each one in the group. Martha is able to cut through any prideful selfishness and keep the wives happy. This becomes her most difficult task. Martha navigates through this task with ease which keeps harmony in George's command staff at camp.

Martha Arrives at Morristown Encampment

In March of 1777, Martha is on her way once again. This time traveling to the Continental Army camp at Morristown. Escort soldiers meet her in Philadelphia to inform her that General Washington is very ill with a throat infection and cold. He has not been able to get out of bed. Martha rushes back into her carriage and arrives at George's bedside on March 15. Martha immediately mixes up her home remedy of onions and a molasses medicinal which in a few days cures the General of his affliction. *In a God moment,* Martha arrives with her prayers and home remedy, and George recovers completely.

On March 30, 1777 General Greene writes to his wife Kitty, wishing she could be with him in camp as Martha is with George:

"Mrs. Washington is extremely fond of the General and he of her; they are very happy in each other."[40]

George Washington Parke Custis writes in 1859:

"Forty years as husband, General Washington retained an old fashioned habit of husbands, as he always did the ease and elegance of old fashioned manners. He wore suspended from his neck by a gold chain, and resting on his bosom, the miniature portrait of his wife, from the time of their marriage until he ceased to live in nature."[41]

Martha Washington's actions in supporting the Revolutionary War, visiting sick and wounded soldiers, praying for them at Continental Army camps, and upholding her husband's large task in leading the Patriot Army to victory, place Martha as a Founder.

Martha, responding clearly to a distant relative who questions George's support for the Patriot cause, states:

"Yes, I foresee consequences, dark days, domestic happiness suspended, social enjoyments abandoned, and eternal separation on earth possible. But my mind is made up, my heart is in the cause. George is right: he is always right. God has promised to protect the righteous and I will trust Him."[42]

****

Chapter Two Questions for Reflection

1. To whom does General Nathanael Greene say he must look for protection in the midst of the war? What does General Greene say about New England virtues?
2. Thomas Jefferson writes in the Declaration of Independence, that *all men are created equal and endowed by their Creator with certain unalienable rights*. What are these rights God gives all men and women that Jefferson points out? What does it mean that these rights are unalienable?
3. Rev. Witherspoon comments that knowledge of God and His truths bring liberty to a nation. Do you agree that true liberty comes from God? See Galatians 5:1a, 2 Corinthians 3:17. Who is really free? See John 8:31-32.
4. Richard Bassett comments that people who believe only in what they can see or touch are foolish. God's power is so much greater. Do you agree? Why or why not?
5. Martha Washington gives hope to many Continental Army soldiers whose path she comes across in her travels. What are the things she does for the sick and wounded soldiers in camp? To whom does Martha say she places the protection of her husband in and the success of the cause of independence?

Chapter Three

Faith in God

We have this treasure in jars of clay to show that this all surpassing power is from God and not from us. We are hard pressed on every side, but not crushed; perplexed, but not in despair; persecuted, but not abandoned; struck down, but not destroyed. 2 Corinthians 4:7-9

George Washington 1732-1799

Member of Congress, Commanding General of the Continental Army during the Revolutionary War, Signer of the U.S. Constitution, First President of the United States, Father of our Country.

George Washington is born on February 22, 1732 at Pope's Creek Farm in Westmoreland County, Virginia to Augustine and Mary Ball Washington. George is the oldest of six children born to this marriage. George has two older half-brothers from Augustine's first marriage to Jane Butler who dies in 1729. Augustine marries Mary Ball on March 6, 1731.

Augustine thrives in land development as well as owning an ironworks thirty miles from his house. Augustine owns slaves. When George is seven years of age, Augustine moves his family to Ferry Farm near Fredericksburg on a ferry crossing on the Rappahannock River. When George is eleven years of age, his father suddenly dies. George inherits slaves and land at Ferry Farm kept in guardianship by his mother until he becomes of legal age. Lawrence, his half-brother inherits Little Hunting Creek farm and older half-brother Austin inherits Pope Creek farm.

Young George Chooses Rules to Govern His Life

With George's father gone, there is no longer money available for a tutor or college. Mary Ball does all she can to survive on sparse income to bring up George and his younger siblings. Mary Ball attends church regularly with her children, and reads the Bible to them daily. Mary Ball is a disciplinarian who sees that her children learn manners, learn to be humble, and learn to be frugal in their living.

George decides as a young teenager what type of person he is going to be. He learns and transcribes the "Rules of Civility" into his own notebook when attending classes at his home church, St. George's Anglican Church in Fredericksburg. George takes these rules to heart to govern civil and personal behavior for his life. George decides his values for life will be honesty, integrity, virtue, tenacity in getting a job done, piety, and giving to charity to help the less fortunate.

By the time he is thirteen years old, George has gone to Little Huntington Creek to live with his half-brother Lawrence who has renamed the farm Mount Vernon. In 1748, George begins his career as a surveyor at the age of sixteen when he takes part in a trip to survey the Shenandoah Valley. He becomes well acquainted with different areas of the frontier. In 1752, Lawrence dies leaving no heirs. George inherits the 2500 acre farm now known as Mount Vernon. That same year, George is appointed as a major in the Virginia militia and serves the next year on duty in the Ohio Valley.

The French and Indian War Begins

In 1755, George is a colonel in the Virginia militia and is assigned to accompany British General Braddock as a staff officer in the French and Indian War. Britain and France are locked in a war in Europe for supremacy which spills over to their American territories. France has control of settlements in Canada and Louisiana and controls the St. Lawrence and Mississippi Rivers. The French have a lucrative Fur Trade from Canada to the Ohio Valley. Britain controls Hudson's Bay, Nova Scotia and the thirteen colonies along the Atlantic coast. Britain also lays claim to the Ohio Valley.

Colonel Washington is with British General Braddock in the campaign to capture Fort Duquesne at the Forks of the Ohio in late April of 1755. Braddock's forces cut their way through the thick forest and thickets and by July are within twelve miles of the fort.

On July 9, 1755, British forces cross the Monongahela River, and trudge forward. The French and their Indian allies attack in flanking parties from the woods. General Braddock is killed in the skirmish. Two horses are shot out from under George. Four bullets whiz through his coat. British soldiers become disoriented and break ranks. George is the only uninjured staff officer and is able to gather the British forces together to retreat. George presides over General Braddock's burial with the reading of scriptures and prayers from his own Anglican Book of Prayer he pulls from his pocket.

George later writes to his brother John Augustine on July 18, 1755:

"As I have heard, since my arriv'l at this place, a circumstantial acct. of my death and dying speech, I take this early opportunity of contradicting the first, and assuring you, that I have not as yet composed the later. By the all-powerful dispensations of Providence, I have been protected beyond all human probability or expectation; for I had four Bullets through my Coat, and two Horses shot under me, and yet escaped unhurt."[43]

Definitely a *God moment* that none of these bullets hit George when the French soldiers and their Indian allies specifically aim rifle shots at all the officers.

George Marries Martha Dandridge Custis

In March 1758, George is on his way to Williamsburg and stops at Poplar Grove to visit Richard Chamberlayne and meets the widow Martha Custis who is there as a guest of the family. This meeting begins their courtship and the pair are wed on January 6, 1759 at Martha's home. The Rev. David Mossom of St. Peter's Anglican Church officiates. George and Martha stay for their honeymoon at her home in New Kent County for a month before Martha and her two children move in at Mount Vernon in Fairfax County.

George and Martha Attend Church

George and Martha attend church on Sundays, weather permitting. When not able to attend church, George reads to Martha in the evening from one of the printed church sermons he has bound into leather volumes in his library. Included in this collection of sermons are John Wesley's messages entitled. "Salvation by Faith", "Original Sin", and "The Almost Christian."

George serves as a vestryman in his home church in Truro Parish for eleven years. This parish includes Pohick, Old Falls, and Alexandria churches. George and Martha partake in Communion at their home church when Communion is given three times a year.

Patsy Parke Custis Dies

George is very fond of his two step-children and is broken-hearted on July 19, 1773, when Pasty Parke Custis, his stepdaughter, becomes ill at the dinner table from what is thought to likely be a seizure. George carries her to her bed and prays for her health. Martha's grandson later tenderly writes:

"Her delicate health, or perhaps her fond affection for the only father she had ever known, so endeared her to the 'general', that he knelt at her dying bed, and with a passionate burst of tears, prayed aloud that her life might be spared, unconscious that even then her spirit had departed."[44]

George Attends the First Continental Congress

In September of 1774, George leaves Mount Vernon to attend the first Continental Congress as a delegate from Virginia. He arrives in Philadelphia before the opening meeting on September 7. George meets with many delegates over dinner and conversation. Delegates are amazed at the depth of knowledge about government, social issues, and military skills George possesses. George has an uncanny ability to size up character and personality traits of the persons he meets. Delegates are surprised he is able to discuss topics with people from all walks of life from back woodsmen, shop owners, scholars to the upper crust of society.

During day sessions, George and his fellow Virginia delegates stand up for liberty and the rights of the citizens of Boston to live in a free city; not with their harbor closed by the British navy and British troops occupying the city by force. George agrees with delegates from New England that slavery needs to be abolished.

George and his neighbor George Mason had already sent a bill on July 18, 1774, to stop the importation of slaves into Virginia. The British crown Governor Dunmore vetoes the bill. George had previously sent a bill passed by the House of Burgesses in 1769 to abolish slavery in the Virginia Colony. That bill is vetoed by the British crown Governor Dinwiddie who is appointed by King George. King George III's policy is to support slavery in the British colonies.

George Is Appointed Commander of the Continental Army

On May 4, 1775, George sets out for the Second Continental Congress meeting in Philadelphia. This meeting opens barely three weeks after the momentous battle at Lexington and Concord. George is elected the commander of the Continental Army.

On June 18, George explains in a letter to Martha his new command:

"It has been determined in Congress, that the whole army raised for the defense of the American cause shall be put under my care...I shall rely, therefore, confidently on that Providence, which has heretofore preserved and been bountiful to me, not doubting that I shall return safe to you in the fall."[45]

Continental Congress declares a day of public Humiliation, Prayer and Fasting be observed by all the colonies on Thursday, July 20, 1775. George gives general orders on July 16, 1775, for army soldiers to attend services on the twentieth:

"...It is therefore strictly enjoin'd on all Officers and Soldiers (not upon duty) to attend Divine Service, at the accustomed places of worship, as well in the Lines, at the Encampments and Quarters; and it is expected, that all those who do go to worship, do take their Arms, Ammunitions and Accoutrements and are prepared for immediate action if called upon."[46]

The Fate of Unborn Millions Depends Upon the Continental Army

In a general order issued July 2, 1776, upon an expected attack by combined British forces, George states:

"The fate of unborn Millions will now depend upon God, on Courage and the Conduct of this army. Our cruel and unrelenting Enemy leaves us no choice but a brave resistance or the most abject submission. This is all we can expect. We have, therefore, to resolve to conquer or die...Let us therefore rely upon the goodness of the Cause, and the aid of the Supreme Being, in whose hands Victory is to animate and encourage us to great and noble Actions..."[47]

George Supports Appointment of Chaplains in the Army

For many years, George has wanted chaplains appointed in militias and the army. He states his wishes to Congress. Congress agrees and authorizes for paid military chaplains to serve in the regiments of the Continental Army in 1776. George issues general orders regarding chaplains on July 9, 1776:

"The Hon. Continental Congress having been pleased to allow a Chaplain to each Regiment, with the pay of Thirty-three dollars and one third per month...The Colonels or commanding officers of each regiment are directed to procure Chaplains accordingly, persons of good characters and exemplary lives, and to see that all inferior officers and soldiers pay them a suitable respect and attend carefully upon religious exercises. The blessings and protection of Heaven are at all times necessary but especially so in times of public distress and danger...The General hopes and trusts that every officer and man will endeavor so to live and act as becomes a Christian soldier defending the dearest rights and liberties of his country."[48]

During his generalship of the Continental Army, George instructs his staff officers that no one is to disturb him for an hour in the early morning and an hour in the late evening. Visitors who arrive during these times are surprised to learn the General is in an hour of prayer. When staff officers look in on George, they find their General kneeling down on one knee, with an open Bible upon his other knee in prayer.

George Believes Morals are Important to Winning the War

George believes morals and upstanding behavior count in order and discipline in the army. He gives orders to stop use of all profane language in army camps and orders to stop all gambling in camp. On May 2, 1778, he issues the following statement:

"While we are zealously performing the duties of good Citizens and soldiers we certainly ought not to be inattentive to the higher duties of Religion. To the distinguished Character of Patriot, it should be our highest Glory to add the more distinguished Character of Christian. The signal Instances of providential Goodness which we have experienced and which have now almost crowned our labours with complete Success, demand from us in a peculiar manner the warmest returns of Gratitude and Piety to the Supreme Author of all Good."[49]

Many a time, George rides onto the battlefield to direct troops as he did at the Battle of Princeton. When George finds a Continental Army line sagging or weakening, he rides in the field of battle to personally direct the troops on the ground, in plain view of British cannon firing at him. His own troops know of George's personal courage under fire. In a *God moment*, George is never shot or hurt seriously on the battlefield.

Whether George is back at Mount Vernon after the Revolutionary War, serving as president of the Constitutional Convention, or in retirement, he continues to be in an hour of prayer each morning and each evening.

George Is Elected the First President of the United States

In his initial Inaugural Address, as the first President of the United States on April 30, 1789, in New York City, George states:

"We ought to be no less persuaded that the propitious smiles of Heaven can never be expected on a nation that disregards the eternal rules of order and right which Heaven itself has ordained..."[50]

As president, George issues a proclamation of the first National Day of Thanksgiving on October 3, 1789. In his Thanksgiving message, George reminds the nation:

"Whereas, it is the duty of all nations to acknowledge the Providence of Almighty God, to obey his will, to be grateful for his benefits and humbly implore his protection and favor,...to recommend to the people of the United States a day of public thanksgiving and prayer, to be observed by acknowledging with grateful hearts the many and signal favors of Almighty God."[51]

In 1797, George laments to his friend Lawrence Lewis:

"I wish from my soul that the Legislature of this state (Virginia) could see the policy of abolition of slavery. It would prevent much future mischief."[52]

As president, George is able to get "An Ordinance of the Territory of the United States Northwest of the River Ohio," passed. George proudly signs this bill into law when it reaches his desk. This law prohibits slavery in any new states that become part of the Union in territory ceded to America by the British at the end of the Revolutionary War.

No measure to abolish slavery passes in the Virginia state legislature. George hopes other slave owners will follow in his path, when in his will George frees his slaves upon his death.

On April 21, 1891 in Philadelphia, George Washington's heirs hold an auction to sell heirlooms from Mount Vernon. One twenty-four page pocketbook containing prayers written in George's distinctive handwriting is found. That George took the time to write these prayers into a personal pocket memorandum book he could carry around with him, means these prayers were important to him.

One prayer written for Monday morning includes these words:

"O Eternal and everlasting God, I presume to present myself this morning before Thy Divine majesty...Thou has given me sweet and pleasant sleep, whereby I find my body refreshed and comforted for performing the duties of the day, in which I beseech Thee to defend me from perils of body and soul. Direct my thoughts, words, and work. Wash away my sins in the immaculate blood of the Lamb. Purge my heart by Thy Holy Spirit, from the dross of my natural corruption that I may with more freedom of mind and liberty of will serve Thee, the everlasting God...daily frame me more and more into thy likeness of Thy Son Jesus Christ, that living in Thy fear, and dying in Thy favor, I may in Thy appointed time attain Thy Resurrection of the just unto eternal life."[53]

****

Lord, you have been our dwelling place through all generations. Before the mountains were born or you brought forth the earth and the world, from everlasting to everlasting you are God. Psalm 90:1-2

John Adams 1735-1826

Lawyer, Member of the Continental Congress, Signer of the Declaration of Independence, Signer of the Bill of Rights, Diplomat, Second President of the United States

John is born on October 30, 1735, in Braintree (now Quincy), Massachusetts to John and Susanna Boylston Adams. John grows up learning very young out of the *New England Primer.*

He is considered a bright capable student and enters Harvard College at age fifteen. John studies mathematics and science under John Winthrop at Harvard. After graduating in 1755, John finds he has interest in law and signs up for law studies for two years under the direction of James Putnam in Worcester. John teaches school during the day in Worcester to fund his way through the two years he is there. John writes in his diary he studies the Bible four days a week. John as a Christian, commits his life to Godly principles of honesty, piety and frugality. In 1758, John completes his law studies and moves back to the farm with his parents. John assists them in their farming chores and attends First Church (Congregational) in Braintree. John's father is a deacon at the church. John is admitted to the bar in 1759 at age twenty-four and begins to practice law in Braintree.

John Marries Abigail Smith

On October 25, 1764, John marries Abigail Smith of Weymouth. They will go on to have four children who live to adulthood. John and Abigail move into the older house on the Adams' farm. Four years later, John moves his family to Boston, as he expands his legal practice.

In the fall of 1770, John defends nine British soldiers at their trial for actions taken in the Boston Massacre. John and his partner, Josiah Quincy, Jr., win acquittals for seven of the soldiers and reduced sentences of manslaughter for the two remaining British defendants.

John is Elected a Delegate to the First Continental Congress

John moves his law offices back to Braintree in June 1774 after being elected as a delegate to Congress. John begins his travel in August to the First Continental Congress. Before reaching Philadelphia, John writes on August 28 from New Jersey to console Abigail:

"Resignation to the Will of Heaven is our only Resource in such dangerous times. Prudence, and Caution shall be our guides. I have the strongest Hope, that We shall yet see a clearer Sky, and better times."[54]

John becomes known for his honesty, and hardworking habits. He is recognized for being brilliant with details and his ability to size up situations. John is very passionate about liberty and has great perseverance in standing up for issues important in gaining independence from Great Britain.

John Is Elected to the Second Continental Congress

On April 1775, the Battle of Lexington and Concord starts the Revolutionary War. John journeys out of Braintree in late April to reach

Philadelphia in early May to attend the second Continental Congress as a delegate from Massachusetts. John is worried about Abigail and responds to one of her letters on July 7, 1775:

"Your Description of the Distresses of the worthy Inhabitants of Boston, and the other Sea Port Towns, is enough to melt a Heart of stone. Our Consolation must be this, my dear, that Cities may be rebuilt, and People reduced to Poverty, may acquire fresh Property: but a Constitution of Government once changed from Freedom, can never be restored. Liberty once lost is lost forever."[55]

John feels honesty, faithfulness and integrity before God count in one's personal and public life. John further believes that principles of truth, honesty and faithfulness before God apply to national policies and decisions.

John recounts America's place in heaven's will to Abigail in a letter dated July 3, 1776:

"Britain has been fill'd with Folly, and America with Wisdom, at least that is my judgement. Time must determine. It may be the Will of Heaven, that the two Countries should be sundered forever. It may be the Will of Heaven that America shall suffer Calamities still more wasting and Distresses yet more dreadfull. If this is to be the Case, it will have this good Effect, at least: it will inspire Us with many Virtues, which we have not, and correct many Errors, Follies and Vices, which threaten to disturb, dishonor and destroy Us."[56]

After the Declaration of Independence is passed by Congress, John describes the momentous event to Abigail in a letter:

"The second day of July 1776, will be the most memorable Epoch in the history of America. I am apt to believe that it will be celebrated, by succeeding Generations, as the great anniversary Festival. It ought to be commemorated, as the Day of Deliverance by solemn Acts of Devotion to God Almighty."[57]

John continues to serve his country abroad as a commissioner for France and the Netherlands, and as an ambassador to Great Britain after the war. He is elected twice as vice-president of the U.S. serving with President George Washington.

John is Elected the Second President of the United States

On February 8, 1797, John is elected the second President of the United States. John and Abigail continue to reside in Philadelphia until November 1, 1800. John moves into the presidential residence in Washington, D.C. The house is unfinished. John sets up his office and uses the back stairs (the only stairs up yet) to get up to his bedroom at night. John shares this prayer with Abigail in a letter:

"I pray Heaven to bestow the best blessings on this house and on all that shall hereafter inhabit it. May none but honest and wise men ever rule under this roof"[58]

John's prayer is inscribed into the mantelpiece in the State Dining Room of the White House.

When Abigail moves in two weeks later, she becomes the first First Lady to live in the White House. On January 1, 1801, President John Adams and First Lady Abigail are the first to hold a reception in the second-floor oval room that gives a view of the Potomac River.

In his Inaugural Address on March 4, 1797, John includes this prayer:

"May that Being who is supreme over all, the Patron of Order, the Fountain of Justice, and the Protector in all the ages of the world of virtuous liberty, continue His blessing upon this nation and its Government and give it all possible success and duration consistent with the ends of His providence."[59]

****

Righteousness and justice are the foundation of your throne; love and faithfulness go before you. Blessed are those who have learned to acclaim you, who walk in the light of your presence, O Lord. Psalm 89:14-15

Charles Carroll of Carrollton 1737-1832

Delegate from Maryland to the Second Continental Congress, Signer of the Declaration of Independence, U.S. Senator from Maryland, Maryland State Senator.

Charles Carroll is born on September 19, 1737 in Annapolis, Maryland into a Roman Catholic family. His grandfather Daniel Carroll has emigrated from Ireland to the colony of Maryland under the protection of Lord Baltimore in the late seventeenth century. Daniel is able to begin a tobacco plantation. Charles' father who is Roman Catholic, takes Charles to France at the age of eight years old to study in a Jesuit College at St. Omar's. (There are no Catholic schools in the colonies at this time). Charles studies there for six years then goes onto another Jesuit school of learning at Rheims. After a year at Rheims he goes on to study at the College of Louis le Grand, and graduates when he is seventeen years old.

Charles begins to study law in Paris and then goes to London in 1757 to continue his law studies another six years. Charles visits the English House of Commons many times. He becomes acquainted with how the British Parliament operates and is informed about British attitudes toward the colonies. Charles studies bookkeeping and land surveying at the suggestion of his father who corresponds regularly by mail. Charles' mother dies while he is in London.

At the age of twenty-six years old, Charles returns to Maryland in 1763. By then Charles is fluent in French and English and a very capable horseman. His father gives him Carrollton Manor, a ten thousand acre plantation, in Fredrick County, Maryland. Charles inherits land, tobacco crops and slaves. In June 1768, Charles marries Mary Darnall. They will become parents of six daughters and one son. Only two of the daughters will survive beyond early childhood.

Charles Writes a Newspaper Column as "First Citizen"

Charles keeps abreast of all the political issues of the day, especially taxation of Maryland and the other colonies by the British. Charles does not speak out right away on his ideas and feelings because Catholics are disdained in the colonies. Anti-Catholic attitudes are especially strong in New England resulting from persecution the early Puritans suffered under the reigns of King James I and King Charles I (both Catholic kings). Many Puritans left England in 1630 to come to Massachusetts for religious freedom. The Pilgrims left earlier arriving in 1620 at Plymouth Rock.

By 1773, taxation issues with the British are so vexing Charles can no long keep his opinions private. He begins publishing a column in the *Maryland Gazette* and signs it "First Citizen."

Charles writes fervently against British taxation of commerce, British policy that colonists can buy goods only from British companies, and the additional taxes on tea and sugar. So eloquent is Charles' writing that citizens of the Annapolis area are amazed and want to know who is "First

Citizen." Once people find out it is Charles writing these articles, he becomes one of the leading voices for freedom from Britain in Maryland.

Ire Against British Policies Increases

In 1774, Charles is named as one of a committee of forty-four persons who are in charge to enforce the resolution of Congress against British imports is followed. Charles is also appointed to the Committee of Safety for the city.

On October 15, 1774, the *Peggy Stewart*, a ship owned by a local merchant, arrives in the port of Annapolis with 2,330 pounds of British tea on board. Irate citizens of Annapolis turn out to protest and the Non-Import Association votes to burn the ship. Charles is consulted about legal authority to burn the ship. Charles agrees the association has legal authority so the ship and its cargo are burned.

Charles is Appointed to a Commission to Represent Congress in Canada

In 1776, Charles is appointed by the Continental Congress to join a commission to represent Congress in Canada. The other two commissioners are Ben Franklin and Samuel Chase. Charles is chosen for his executive skills, ability to speak French, and because he is Roman Catholic. Charles asks his cousin, Father John Carroll, a Catholic priest, to accompany them to assist in representing the colonies and their cause of independence from Britain. The commissioners hope to travel to Montreal and Quebec City.

Upon arriving in northern New York, Charles finds out the Continental Army is short of supplies, and therefore, not able to launch an immediate attack against the British in Canada.

Local merchants are upset as they are owed money the army has not been able to pay them for goods and services rendered. In Montreal, Charles and the others learn the British are shoring up defenses in the whole province of Quebec. Taking Canada will not be easy. The commissioners write a letter to Congress to pay the bills the army owes and then return home at the end of their meeting.

Charles Is a Delegate to the Second Continental Congress

Upon return to Maryland, Charles is elected a delegate to represent Maryland at the Second Continental Congress. Charles arrives in time to sign the Declaration of Independence. Charles signs as Charles Carroll of Carrollton to identify which Charles Carroll of Maryland is signing the document. There are several other distant cousins and relatives of the same name. By doing so, Charles puts his life and fortune literally on the line. Charles cites his main reason for joining the Patriot cause is for religious freedom.

Charles is a good friend of George Washington who comes to Annapolis from time to time on business. Charles and George join together in a business enterprise to establish a new water way to the North and West for shipping their goods from Maryland and Virginia.

Once Charles is a delegate in Philadelphia, General Washington writes the Congress to place Charles on the Foreign Applications Committee so Charles can be in the know of what foreign officers are coming to the Americans to fight with them. Charles is very capable, able to speak French, and is very adept at interviewing the French officers who come to the colonies. Charles keeps General Washington informed of who is asking for commands in the Continental Army. At this time, it is Congress who appoints commanders, not the army itself.

Charles and the Conway Cabal

Charles serves on the Board of War and keeps General Washington duly informed of any issues or problems that arise. One such situation becomes known as the Conway Cabal. The Board of War tries to cut down on desertions, increase the timeliness of army supplies getting to the troops, and improve training of troops.

General Horatio Gates recommends to several of his close friends in Congress that Thomas Conway be appointed Army Inspector General. Congress promotes Conway to major general. General Horatio Gates who wins the Battle of Saratoga and General Mifflin are appointed to the Board of War. Gates would like to be the Commander of the Army himself. All three, Conway, Gates and Mifflin lobby Congress to get rid of General Washington. Charles keeps tabs on what is going on and visits Valley Forge to talk to General Washington. Washington contacts Henry Laurens the President of Congress about the matter and sends General Greene to represent keeping him in command. General Gates who wants to replace Washington is not appointed, General Conway is reassigned to another army post in New York, and General Thomas Mifflin who is Quartermaster General resigns from the army. General Washington stays as the Commander of the Continental Army throughout all the Revolutionary War.

During the war, Charles gives financial aid to General Washington and the Continental Army for supplies at Valley Forge, Yorktown, and later in support of the American Navy.

Charles' Personal Life

Charles suffers tragedy in his personal life in 1782, when his father falls from a porch and dies of his injuries a few days later. Charles' wife Mary dies the same year when she is thirty five years old. Charles is left to raise his children alone. He never remarries.

In 1788, Charles resigns from Congress to return to Maryland where he serves as a senator in the Maryland legislature. In his capable leadership, he is able to advise both houses of the legislature to work together and support their new state constitution which he helped to write. As he becomes more involved in the cause of freedom, Charles realizes that slavery is wrong. He states:

"Why keep alive the question of slavery? It is admitted to by all to be a great evil."[60]

Charles frees many slaves over the years and celebrates his birthday at eighty by freeing thirty slaves.

On the fiftieth anniversary of the signing of the Declaration of Independence, Charles writes in 1826:

"Grateful to Almighty God for the blessings which, through Jesus Christ our Lord, He has conferred on this beloved country in her emancipation and on myself in permitting me, under circumstances of mercy to survive the fiftieth year of independence adopted by Congress on 4th July 1776, which I originally subscribed on the 2nd day of August of the same year and of which I am now the last surviving signer."[61]

****

It is God who arms me with strength and makes my way perfect. Psalm 18:32

James Madison 1751-1836

Member of Virginia Council, Member of the Continental Congress, Member of the Constitutional Convention, Secretary of State, Fourth President of the United States, Father of the U.S. Constitution

James is born March 16, 1751 at Port Conway, Virginia. His father James Sr. and mother Nelly are visiting his mother at the time. His parents live at Mount Pleasant in a simple frame farm house in the Piedmont region of Virginia. James is the eldest child and is taught to read and write by his mother and grandmother. James is born into a devout family and grows up in the Anglican Church. His father serves as a vestryman and the family attends church regularly.

At age eleven James attends a boarding school with other boys from the Piedmont area. The instructor is Donald Robertson, an immigrant from Scotland, whom James comes to admire and who instills in James the love of learning. Instructor Robertson has an extensive library of such authors as Virgil and Cicero, and modern writers of the time, such as Locke and Montesquieu. Locke and Montesquieu propose that freedom is a right of every citizen. James also studies Latin, Greek, French, geography, algebra and geometry.

James' father builds a larger house about a third of a mile from the old farm house as the family has grown to six children. James' father hires a live in tutor named Thomas Martin, a recent graduate from the College of New Jersey, to teach his children. James is enthused about attending the same college and leaves home when he is eighteen years old to study there.

James Graduates from the College of New Jersey

James fits well into the College of New Jersey and excels at his classes. He finishes his undergraduate studies and stays another year to study theology and ethics with Rev. Witherspoon, a Presbyterian minister. James is so happy with his classes and Rev. Witherspoon's instruction, he contemplates going into the ministry. James graduates from the College of New Jersey (later known as Princeton University) in 1772. James strains his health by cramming two years of study into one as an under graduate, and then graduate school. Instead of going into the ministry, James is exhausted and returns home.

James Begins His Government Service in Virginia

James is elected to the Orange County Committee of Safety in 1775 with his father as the committee leader. James works to support the boycott of British goods and the start of local militias. James being of slim build, five feet six inches tall, and about one hundred ten pounds, is not physically sturdy enough to join as a soldier in the Continental Army or local militia.

In 1776, James is appointed to the Virginia Constitutional Convention and helps write the state's new constitution. James supports George Mason's bill of rights and sees it becomes part of the new constitution. In 1778, James is appointed to Patrick Henry's Council for the State of Virginia. Virginia's state constitution forbids any governor from vetoing legislation. The governor can act only with the consent of an eight member council. James learns much about the conditions of the Continental Army's lack of supplies, and hardships through General Washington's correspondence with Governor Henry. Governor Henry dispatches supplies of meat, salt, and grain whenever he can to the Continental Army. James learns about the working relationship, in time of war, between military and civilian leaders, about army promotions, court-martials, deaths, and the need to keep new Virginia recruits coming to fight.

Being on the Governor's Council, James lives in Williamsburg where he comes into direct contact with administration issues and politics. James learns quickly how to cultivate needed relationships with others to get problems solved.

In 1780-1783, James is a delegate to the Congress of Confederation. James's ability to study a situation, decide on a course of action, and his canny talent to come up with a step by step process for resolution of a problem becomes well-known. From 1784-1786, James serves in the Virginia state legislature.

James Pulls Together the Constitutional Convention in Philadelphia

James and Alexander Hamilton set up a meeting of delegates from each state to discuss trade issues and updates for the confederation. Both James and Alexander Hamilton intend to introduce a new form of government.

Delegates are amazed in Philadelphia when discussing what type of government the United States is to have. James writes down on paper the pros and cons of all types of governments throughout history, from ancient Greeks, to the Romans, and those of older antiquity. James is like a walking encyclopedia of information on all aspects of governmental structure and process.

James meets privately with George Washington first to test out his ideas about what the branches of government would be and what the executive branch might look like. With Washington's support, James recommends three branches of government to the Constitutional Convention.

Isaiah 33:22 becomes the undergirding scripture for dividing governmental power into three branches. Isaiah describes God's power. *For the Lord is our judge* (judicial branch), *the Lord is our lawgiver* (legislative branch), *the Lord is out king* (executive branch), *and it is He who will save us.*

The state of New York is slow to come to an agreement on any kind of new federal national government. The *Federalist Papers* are widely read and successful which discuss the issues of the day in support of a federal national government. James writes twenty-nine of the eighty-five papers. Alexander Hamilton and John Jay write the rest. New York joins in the Constitutional Convention by sending delegates to Philadelphia.

The Northern states are against slavery. Southern delegates from South Carolina, North Carolina and Georgia threaten to withdraw their support for a U.S. Constitution if slavery is voted out. Already a dividing line has formed between North and South. Leaders of the Constitutional Convention, like James Madison, George Washington, and Ben Franklin, know the only way their new nation can survive against European powers in the New World is to be a united country. Britain has control of Canada and interests in the Pacific Northwest which includes Oregon, Washington and parts of western Idaho. France has control of the Louisiana Territory which covers territory from New Orleans up the Mississippi northwest to the Missouri and Platte Rivers. Spain has control of Florida, and large areas of land that will become Texas, and the Southwest to the Pacific Ocean.

James agrees to work on a resolution to try and keep the states united. This is called the Three-Fifths Compromise for representation in the House of Representatives. Southern states by population have many more persons in their states counting all slaves. In their grab for political power, Southern delegates want slaves counted to determine the number of seats their states would get in the House. James is able to see to it Northern states who are against slavery gain more political power by counting slaves as three-fifths. Free Blacks and Whites count as one each when determining the number of House seats per state.

On September 17, 1787, the U.S. Constitution is ratified by the delegates. James writes to Thomas Jefferson who is the American ambassador to France:

"Adding to these considerations, the natural diversity of human opinions on all new and complicated subjects, it is impossible to consider the degree of concord which ultimately prevailed as less than a miracle."[62]

James is Elected to the House of Representatives

In 1789, James is elected to the new House of Representatives. He works very hard in the House and is urged on by fellow Virginians to come up with a bill of rights for the new constitution. James has already worked with Virginia delegates on a Virginia Bill of Rights when he served in the Virginia legislature. This bill stated:

"That religion, or the duty we owe the Creator, and the manner of discharging it, can be directed only by reason and conviction, not by force or violence; and therefore, all men are equally entitled to the free exercise of religion according to the dictates of conscience."[63]

James continues to work closely with President George Washington to get the new government up functioning smoothly. By 1793, Congress is meeting in Philadelphia as the capitol of the new country.

James Meets Dolley Payne Todd

When summer begins, a Yellow Fever epidemic hits Philadelphia. President and Mrs. Washington leave the city. The government shuts down as do many businesses. Thousands of citizens flee the city away from the swamps that surround it. On October 13, 1793, John Todd, a Quaker lawyer, dies from the fever as well as his parents and baby son. This leaves his grieving widow, Dolley Payne Todd with one surviving son, John Payne Todd. Congress does return to Philadelphia in November and the city is declared safe from Yellow Fever.

Out walking in the city one spring day, James sees Dolley on the street. James makes arrangements to be introduced to her. By August 1794, James and Dolley have set their wedding date. They are married on September 15, 1794 at Harewood, the home of Lucy and George Steptoe Washington.

James serves out his term in the House of Representatives and retires back home on March 4, 1797. By this time, James' father is ill and requires much more help in running the farm.

With additions onto the house to accommodate them, James and Dolley move in permanently. It appears their time serving in the national government is over as their party is out of power. They call their updated home Montpelier. In January of 1800, James Sr. dies leaving Montpelier farm and one hundred slaves. James is named executor of his father's will. James and his brother William inherit land and slaves.

James Becomes Secretary of State

After Thomas Jefferson is elected president, James and Dolley travel back to Washington, D.C. in March of 1801 to stay at the White House for three weeks. James becomes Jefferson's Secretary of State. James and Dolley find lodging on Pennsylvania Avenue two blocks from the White House. James and Dolley make new friends in the capital and hold charitable events at home. Dolley invites persons from all political persuasions, local residents, and foreign visitors to her table. Dolley invites men and women and is able to blend entertainment at her house into a rousing success. James, being short of stature and shy, has difficulty in meeting people in large groups. At home entertaining, Dolley is able to introduce James to several people at a time. James becomes Dolley's charming escort.

Dolley creates a political culture in Washington, D.C. So likeable is Dolley, that their friend, Thomas Jefferson, invites Dolley to be the hostess at larger dinner parties in the White House.

James oversees, as Secretary of State, the purchase of the Territory of Louisiana from Napoleon in 1803. James supports the acquisition of the land which opens up the mouth of the Mississippi River to American trade.

James Is Elected the Fourth President of the United States

James is elected the fourth President of the United States on March 4, 1809. In his first inaugural address, James tells the American people:

"But the source to which I look or the aids which alone can supply my deficiencies is in the well-tried intelligence and virtue of my fellow-citizens, and in the counsels of those representing them in the other departments associated in the care of the national interests.

In these my confidence will under every difficulty be best placed, next that which we have all been encouraged to feel in the guardianship and guidance of that Almighty Being whose power regulates the destiny of nations, whose blessings have been so conspicuously dispensed to this rising Republic, and to whom we are bound to address our devout gratitude for the past, as well as our fervent supplications and best hopes for the future."[64]

Soon after James becomes president, Great Britain and France increase their shipping interests to interfere with those of the United States. Any action Congress takes or puts forward to enhance trade, angers either side. This breaks out into the War of 1812.

The British Army Attacks the Capitol and Burns the White House

On August 22, 1814, the British Army invades Maryland and then heads toward Washington, D.C. By the next morning, James receives messages the American troops are at Bladensburg waiting the British. James leaves to assess troop movements in Maryland.

Dolley is concerned as she watches from the White House balcony for any news from James. Dolley has her carriage ready. Seeing American militiamen retreating in the afternoon, Dolley has the White House servants load up James' cabinet papers, silver sets, and favorite books into a wagon. By three o'clock in the afternoon, Dolley secures another wagon, and has servants load up other valuables from the house.

Charles Carroll stops by to urge Dolley to leave the White House immediately as the British Army has broken through American lines. Dolley insists on taking the Gilbert Stuart portrait of President George Washington with her. Charles Carroll leaves to return to the field to check on James.

Dolley describes in her letter to Lucy Todd, her sister, on August 23, 1814, how difficult it is to unscrew the portrait from the wall:

"This process was found to be too tedious for these perilous moments; I have ordered the frame broken, and the canvass taken out, it is done, and the precious portrait placed in the hands of two gentlemen from New York, for safe keeping. And now, dear sister, I must leave this house, or the retreating army will make me a prisoner in it."[65]

Dolley is anxious for James and his safety. She continues in her letter to Lucy Todd,

"Mr. Madison comes not, may God protect him."[66]

At midnight a messenger from General Armstrong's command arrives and orders Dolley to clear out of the White House as the American Army is in retreat. Charles Carroll returns a second time and drives Dolley out in her carriage, followed by staff driving the carefully packed wagons on to Georgetown. There they cross the river to Bell Vue, one of Charles' estates.

James eventually returns to an empty White House. James sends messages on to Dolley to meet him at Wiley's Inn near Great Falls, Virginia. As James and several of his staff cross over the Potomac River into Virginia, the British Army enters capital and sets fire to the Capitol Building and to the White House on August 24. British officers feel they have struck a great blow by burning Washington, D.C. Peace negotiations have already begun in Ghent, Belgium between British and American diplomats, but word has not reached the troops in the field.

Day of Thanksgiving Proclaimed

On March 4, 1815, after the war has ended, a peace treaty is signed. James recommends a Day of Thanksgiving be observed by the people of the United States and proclaims to Congress:

"No people ought to feel greater obligations to celebrate the goodness of the Great Disposer of Events and the Destiny of Nations than the people of the United States...He protected and cherished them under all difficulties and trials to which they were exposed in their early days. Under His fostering care their habits, their sentiments and their pursuits prepared them for a transition in due time to a state of independence and self-government...It is for blessings such as these, and more especially for the restoration of the blessing of peace, that I now recommend that the second day of April next be set apart as a day on which the people of every religious denomination may in their solemn assemblies unite their hearts and voices in a freewill offering to our Heavenly Benefactor of their homage of thanksgiving and songs of praise."[67]

Both the House of Representatives and the Senate pass the above proposal and proclaim:

"That a day may be recommended to be observed by the people of the United States with religious solemnity as a day of thanksgiving and of devout acknowledgements of Almighty God for His great goodness manifested in restoring to them the blessings of peace."[68]

****

Chapter Three Questions for Reflection

1. We live in such a self-centered age that does not understand humility. George Washington gives up absolute military and political power twice in his life. When did he do this? What virtues does George decide as a young teen were most important for his life? What does George say we owe back to God for His goodness and protection over us as a nation?
2. When John Adams is asked if America can win the struggle against Great Britain, what is John's answer? John felt strongly that true integrity of a person's character is important both in his or her private life as well as his or her public life. Do you agree? Why or why not? What advice does John give for living in dangerous times as an individual citizen and as a nation?
3. To whom does Charles Carroll of Carrollton state he feels grateful for the many blessings given to him and to his beloved country, the United States, on the fiftieth anniversary of the signing of the Declaration of Independence?

4. James Madison advocates freedom of religion for each person. James states the unalienable right of every person to exercise freedom of religion is also a duty to God (the Creator). Do you agree? Why or why not? What does James describe that God has done for the people of the United States?
5. James Madison once indicated during discussions about the slave states during the Constitutional Convention that he hoped slavery would go out of business in twenty years. In the late 1700's, many plantations in the South were struggling to make ends meet. Low crop prices, intensive work needed to raise tobacco, rice, indigo, and the depletion of the soil did not give a bright future for the industry. James Madison, like many other leaders of the country, believed in the rule of law as paramount in the founding of the new nation. It is very difficult for us with our 21st century values and mind set to understand James Madison's actions. The slave trade was not abolished by Congress until 1808 with the passage of a bill to do so. President Jefferson signed this bill into law. This did not end the hideous institution of slavery in America that was established in 1619 under British rule. What options do you think James Madison and other leaders could have taken, without the cooperation of Southern states, to end slavery once for all?

Chapter Four

Love in God

Give thanks to the Lord, for he is good; his love endures forever. I Chronicles 16:34

Haym Salomon 1740-1785

Financier of the Continental Army and Continental Congress

Haym is born in Lissa, Poland in 1740. His parents are Jewish refugees from Portugal and his father is a rabbi. From 1025 A.D. through the sixteenth century, Poland is the most tolerant country in Europe toward the Jewish people.

Haym is a very eager student who finds learning languages easy. He speaks his native Polish, German, French, and teaches himself English.

As a young man twenty years old, Haym travels in Europe to work with some of the leading financial bankers in commerce. He learns the brokerage business as well as buying and trading goods off ships. This experience will become very significant later on as he becomes one of the most important financiers for the American cause of independence.

Haym returns home in 1770 when wars in Poland break out with rival neighboring states. In 1772, Poland is petitioned between Prussia, Russia and Austria. The Jewish people come under severe persecution. Haym leaves his parents and sibs to travel to England that same year. He finds work in a brokerage firm and earns enough money to sail to America. He arrives in New York City in August 1772. Haym begins his own brokerage business and becomes well known for his hard work, honesty and integrity. He is not able to join the Jewish synagogue in the city because the British have shut its doors and boarded up the building.

Haym Becomes a Spy for General Washington

Haym meets Isaac Sears and other members of the New York Sons of Liberty through his business and joins their cause. In 1773, the Sons of Liberty proclaim their opposition against the British Tea act by taking measures to enforce the embargo on any British tea being sold in the colonies. Isaac Sears and other Sons of Liberty stop the unloading of British ships carrying tea in New York City harbor.

Haym works as an agent for General Washington. By speaking German, he is able to gather information from Hessian soldiers who are quartered in the city. This includes details about troop movements, troop strength and plans. Another agent, Hercules Mulligan is a tailor in the city. Hercules picks up bits of military plans from British soldiers who are getting their uniforms fitted. Hercules and Haym send on their information directly to General Washington.

In 1776, the British arrest Haym for being a spy and hold him as a prisoner on board a boat with Hessian mercenaries. He continues his mission of speaking to Hessians who are prisoners. He talks many of them out of fighting for the British once they are freed. He is released after eighteen months.

Once Haym is out of prison, he is back building up his business which includes shipping supplies through privateers to Continental Army lines. In 1777, Haym marries Rachel Franks, the daughter of a New York merchant. They will go on to have four children.

In August 1778, Haym is once again accused by the British of being a spy and is charged in a plot to blow up British ships and warehouses in New York City. He is taken to Provost Prison and locked up by British General Clinton. Clinton asks him who is going to take care of his wife Rachel and their child. Haym responds,

"God will protect them."[69]

Haym figures out a way to pay the guards to get out of jail. He and his family escape to Philadelphia.

Haym Meets Robert Morris in Philadelphia

In Philadelphia, Haym begins a new business as a commission broker dealing in the sale of bills of exchange. Haym meets Robert Morris who runs Willig-Morris & Company. The two join together in their fund raising efforts to support General Washington and the Continental Army. Both men have extensive contacts in overseas trade.

Haym joins the governing council of synagogue Mikveh Israel and continues to give generous donations. Haym becomes the treasurer of Ezrath Orechim, a Jewish society for indigent travelers. Haym and Rachel move in to live above Haym's business office on Front Street in the city.

Haym Buys Supplies for the Continental Army

Haym gives funds to Thomas Jefferson, James Madison and James Monroe to pay for their lodging in Philadelphia through the years when they are attending the Continental Congress.

Through his shipping connections with Morris, Haym negotiates the majority of weapons and clothing supplies obtained for the Continental Army from France by way of the West Indies. Hyam gives twenty thousand dollars to General Washington for supplies for the Battle of Yorktown. Robert Morris mentions in his diary from 1781-1784 the assistance that Haym gave him in seventy-five different financial transactions on behalf of the Continental Congress. Haym contributes in all over six hundred thousand dollars to the cause of American liberty.

Haym prays gratefully to God when a privateer ship comes into the Philadelphia port. The ship is rich in cargo which Haym can sell for a profit. He already has pledged support without a cent in the bank to help build a new place of worship. Haym relies on God to provide.

Haym is very familiar with oppression of Jews in parts of Europe. He knows the hardship of Jews in other parts of the world where their crops and houses are burned. Haym does not worry about financial hardships in America. His commitment is to the Patriot cause for religious freedom and a future for his children.

Rachel is worried about Haym's overwork and declining health. He responds to her saying,

"Selfishness only, I believe, is a sin that God finds too difficult to forgive."[70]

On January 5, 1785, Haym dies from tuberculosis that he caught while prisoner on a British ship during the war. Rachel gives birth to their fourth child three months after Haym dies. Shel is left destitute with no way to recover any of the funds Haym has loaned out. Eventually, Rachel remarries to David Helbrun from New York City.

****

Let the word of Christ dwell in you richly as you teach and admonish one another with all wisdom, and as you sing psalms, hymns and spiritual songs with gratitude in your hearts to God. Colossians 3:16

Noah Webster 1758-1843

Revolutionary War Soldier, Lawyer, Author,
Teacher, Schoolmaster of America

On October 16, 1758, the fourth child of Noah and Mercy Webster is born on a farm in West Hartford, Connecticut. This child is a boy whom his father gives his own first name, Noah. Noah Sr. is a descendent of Connecticut's founding governor, John Webster. Baby Noah's mother is a direct descendent of Governor William Bradford of Plymouth Colony. Noah grows up in a Puritan family and local community of Bible believing, church going farmers.

Mercy is a very able teacher who makes sure her children learn to read the Bible, to recite the Lord's Prayer and the Apostles Creed. She instructs her children in family history of the Pilgrims coming to America for religious freedom. Mercy is outgoing, and a positive woman who enjoys giving her children music lessons in singing and playing the flute. Noah shows a special interest in the flute and soon is able to play the instrument as well as sing hymns.

Being part of a farm community, the Webster children grow up with farm chores as well as assisting with planting and harvesting seasons. The community school is open eight to twelve weeks of the year during the months the children are not needed for farm work. Noah would later say his elementary school teachers were so frugally paid and unequipped, the school books so uninviting, and the school house so cold and unappealing, it was difficult to concentrate on much of anything at school.

Noah grows up learning that one's individual success is gauged by a personal work ethic, good moral behavior, church attendance, and helping one's neighbor in need. His young childhood is spent during the close of the French and Indian War, and his teen years during the taxation policies of the British Crown deciding that Americans have to pay for all British costs to maintain the colonies. Noah is twelve years old when the Boston Massacre takes place. British soldiers fire upon an angry mob in Boston and kill five people. Puritan feelings run high in Hartford against the British.

The Puritan Congregational Church in town is where after worship services, citizens in town discuss British taxes, colonial response to the growing subjugation by King George III over the colonies, and support for local militias. As Noah reaches his teens, he is allowed to stay for these discussions.

In 1772, Noah Sr. decides he can afford to send one of his children to college. Noah is chosen as he has shown a love for study and books. His father places Noah under the care of Rev. Nathan Perkins to give Noah preparatory studies to enter college.

Noah Enters Yale College

In 1774, Noah has completed his preparatory studies and enters Yale College in New Haven.

Noah continues his vigorous lessons in Latin, Greek, algebra, botany, physics, philosophy, literature, composition and Bible studies. Noah is a voracious reader and joins the Brothers of Unity who have a large library of several hundred books. Noah becomes acquainted with the ideas of Greek philosophers as well as English authors Locke and Bacon. In science, Noah reads Isaac Newton.

In 1775, Noah is too young to join the New Haven militia who go off to fight the British after the Battle of Lexington and Concord on April 19. Noah stays behind with the young students to work on building up army defenses around the college. Noah continues in daily military drills. When General Lee and his army arrive in New Haven on their way to Boston, General Lee is impressed with the drills of these young students at the college.

On the morning of April 29, 1775, the Yale students march to New Haven green to see the Continental Army off. Noah plays on his flute for the assembled group, *Yankee Doodle Dandy,* as the soldiers march out of town.

Noah Joins the West Hartford Militia

Noah returns home between studies in 1777 to join the West Hartford militia with his father who is a captain and leader of the militia. The militia marches two days to the east bank of the Hudson River to confront the British and keep General Burgoyne from joining up with British forces in New York City. Fortunately British forces under Burgoyne are defeated at the Battle of Saratoga. Noah and his father travel back home unharmed.

Noah Graduates from Yale

Noah returns to Yale to find that Ezra Stiles is the new president of the school. Stiles is a dynamic individual who takes over the education for the senior class. Noah graduates in September 1778 with a Bachelor of Arts degree.

After graduation, Noah returns home to find his father is broke and in debt. Part of the debt is the cost of Noah's college education; the other part is inflation of continental money during the war. Noah's father gives him his last eight dollars and tells Noah he is now on his own.

Noah Becomes a Teacher and Studies Law

Noah states he is anxious about being on his own. The only job he can find is as a teacher at the West Hartford school he attended as a boy. Noah moves around for several months as a school master at various schools. In 1779, Noah is hired by the Brick School in Hartford proper. Noah is boarded with Oliver Ellsworth, a well-known lawyer. Noah begins his law studies. Noah continues to teach at various schools during the day and study law in evenings for a couple of years. He is admitted to the bar in 1781.

Noah Publishes His First Spelling Book

Noah starts work on his first spelling book as he realizes that current school books are deficient in both method and content. Noah is the first American educator to spell words as Americans speak the language. For example, colour becomes color, labour becomes labor, and publick becomes public. Noah groups spelling words together that are spelled out and sound alike. For example: back, hack, jack and lack. Noah devises games and rhymes for children to learn their alphabet and spelling.

Noah obtains support from former Yale friends, including President Ezra Stiles. Noah wants to title his book, *The American Speller.* President

Stiles thinks that title is too mundane to catch on. So the book title becomes, *A Grammatical Institute of the English Language, Comprising an Easy, Concise, and Systematic Method of Education Designed for the Use of English Schools in America*. The book is published in 1783.

While practicing law, Noah travels across the colonies to the larger towns on speaking engagements to sell his new spelling book. He is soon writing a second reading book containing American history, patriotic stories, poetry and a moral catechism. In this catechism students are asked:

"What is moral virtue? It is an honest upright conduct in all our dealings with men."[71]

Noah goes on to explain the most important duties of moral virtue are summed up in Christ's Sermon on the Mount in the gospel of Matthew, Chapter 5. Other topics on morality include: humility, mercy, purity of heart, gratitude, generosity, truth and justice.

Noah's marketing abilities, public advertisements, and speaking tours are a success. His books become widely known and begin to make their way into the school curriculum of the day. Out of the proceeds of his book sales, Noah gives money to several anti-slavery societies.

Noah Becomes Friends with Ben Franklin

In 1785, Noah expands his speaking engagements to Philadelphia where he meets Ben Franklin and begins a friendship in which Franklin funds the printing of new editions of Noah's spelling and grammar books.

That same year, Noah publishes *Sketches of American Policy* which supports development of a new American constitution. Noah visits with George Washington at Mount Vernon to discuss his ideas about the new constitution and gives Washington a copy of his book. *Sketches of*

American Policy becomes widely read across the colonies and is influential in swaying opinion in support of a new constitution.

On April 13, 1787, Noah obtains a teaching job at the Protestant Episcopal Academy in Philadelphia. In May, the Constitutional Convention begins meeting in the same city to formulate a new government for the United States. Noah is available at evening discussions of the delegates who want to discuss his ideas from his book. Noah becomes acquainted with leaders from all thirteen states.

Noah updates his spelling book and publishes it with a new title, *The American Spelling Book,* with the support of Ben Franklin. Noah updates his reading book with fifty pages of historical background on the founding of the United States. Noah's book is successful enough he is able to repay his father for his college expenses at Yale.

Noah Marries and Returns to Connecticut

On October 26, 1789, Noah marries Rebecca Greenleaf who is the daughter of William Greenleaf who is a successful merchant from Boston, and also sheriff of Suffolk County in Massachusetts. Noah and Rebecca settle in West Hartford, Connecticut where Noah begins his law practice to earn money to support his family and the publishing of new editions of his spelling and reading books. Noah and Rebecca will go on to have eight children.

In one of his books, Noah teaches about God and prayer:

"God governs the world in infinite wisdom...Prayer is a duty, but it is in vain to pray without a sincere desire of the heart to obtain what we pray for; to repeat the words of a prayer, without much desire, is solemn mockery."[72]

Noah Publishes His First Dictionary

In 1806, Noah publishes his first dictionary. This is the 40,000 word *Compendious Dictionary of the American Language.* In this dictionary Noah continues his reform of the English language to American use of pronunciation and spelling.

That same year, Noah meets Rev. Moses Stuart who becomes the new pastor of New Haven's First Congregational Church. Stuart is also a graduate of Yale and is a very outgoing preacher whose words greatly inspire all who hear him. Not unlike George Whitfield, who brought many to Christ in an earlier generation, Rev. Stuart is part of the Second Great Awakening and brings many more by faith and renewed faith to Christ.

Noah hears Stuart's preaching and rededicates his life to God. From then on, Noah sets time aside for prayers three times a day. This he does for the rest of his life. With a renewed relationship to God, Noah finds he has inspiration to start a modern language edition of the Bible. Taking his experience and skills learned in putting together his dictionaries, Noah begins work on an updated version of the Bible written in American English. He publishes this revised Bible in 1833.

Noah comments on the Bible:

"All the miseries and evils which men suffer from vice, crime, ambition, injustice, oppression, slavery, and war, proceed from their despising or neglecting the precepts contained in the Bible."[73]

Noah feels so strongly about freedom in society, he points out the origin of civil liberty in his history books for students in schools:

"The religion which has introduced civil liberty is the religion of Christ and His apostles which enjoins humility, piety, and benevolence; which acknowledges every person a brother or a sister, and a citizen with equal rights. This is genuine Christianity, and to this we owe our free constitutions of government."[74]

Continuing with his daily prayers, Noah writes them down in a diary. At the family dinner table one day, Noah shares one of his prayers with Rebecca and the children:

"And may this family be the special care of thy providence. Wilt thou watch over it & all its interests. Preserve all its members in safety. May our hearts be knit together in love to each other, & may we live in nearness to God, and enjoy the consolations of thy Grace. Most gracious God, we commit our way to thee, trusting ourselves & our interests, spiritual & temporal to thy mercy in Jesus Christ."[75]

****

For God so loved the world that he gave his one and only Son, that whoever believes in him shall not perish but have eternal life. John 3:16.

Rev. Richard Allen 1760-1831

Evangelist, Abolitionist, Educator, Writer, Founder of the African Methodist Episcopal Church, First Black Bishop in the United States

Richard is born a slave on February 14, 1760 on one of the plantations of Benjamin Chew of Philadelphia. As a seven year old, Richard, his mother and father and siblings are sold to another plantation owner whose land is near Dover, Delaware. The new owner is Stokeley Sturgis. Richard comments on his family:

"My mother and father lived with him for many years. He was brought into difficulty, not being able to pay for us; and mother having several children after he had bought us, he sold my mother and three children."[76]

This left Richard with an older brother and a sister on the Dover plantation. Richard continues to work the ground, planting and harvesting crops on Sturgis land. Richard describes Stokeley as a humane man who let his slaves attend religious meetings every other Thursday evening.

Richard Allen Is Converted to Christ

In 1777, when seventeen years old, Richard attends a Methodist Society meeting and hears the preaching of Freeborn Garretson. Richard is converted to Christ. Richard describes the experience:

"One night I thought hell would be my portion. I cried unto Him who delighteth to hear the prayers of a poor sinner; and all of a sudden my dungeon shook, my chains flew off, and glory to God, I cried. My soul was filled...Now my confidence was strengthened that the Lord, for Christ's sake heard my prayers, and pardoned my sins."[77]

Methodism is a new gathering of Christians in America. Not recognized as a formal church, Methodists gather in society meetings out in the open, or at people's homes, or at camp meetings. Following the teachings of their founder John Wesley, Methodists minister to the down and out and the least with a fervor to convert all to Christ. Early Methodists preach the Bible and believe that slavery is wrong and always will be wrong.

Richard Allen Receives His Freedom

Sometime after this, Richard asks his master if he can ask some of the Methodist preachers to come and preach at the plantation house. John Gray, the Methodist Society class leader comes to preach the next Wednesday. Freeborn Garrison comes to preach some months later and during this worship service, Stokeley Sturgis is convicted in his spirit that slavery is wrong. Shortly after this, Stokeley arranges for Richard and his brother to buy their time by paying him two thousand dollars in Continental money. Richard takes on extra jobs such as wood chopping and carrying salt to the Continental Army. Richard becomes a free man in 1780.

Richard comments about the Lord and his freedom:

"I had it often impressed upon my mind that I should one day enjoy freedom; for slavery is a bitter pill, notwithstanding we had a good master... But I have reason to bless my dear Lord that a door was opened unexpectedly for me to buy my time, and enjoy my libery."[78]

Rev. Allen Begins Preaching the Gospel

Richard begins traveling around Delaware, New Jersey, Maryland and Pennsylvania preaching the gospel at camp meetings and Methodist Society gatherings. In 1784, Richard attends the Christmas Conference in Baltimore during which the Methodist Episcopal Church is founded in America and Francis Asbury is ordained Bishop for the people called Methodist in the United States. Richard receives his orders to preach at this conference and is officially recognized as a Methodist minister.

In 1786, Richard becomes a preacher at St. George's Methodist Episcopal Church in Philadelphia and preaches at the five o' clock services. St. George's Church begins to grow with increasing numbers of blacks and whites attending. Richard preaches to people in the church, and to people in other places up to four or five times a day.

With more black people coming into St. George's Church, the trustees build a balcony in the sanctuary. One day Richard Allen and Absalom Jones sit in their usual pew to pray. Church trustees, brushing aside Christ's teaching to *love your neighbor as yourself* (Matthew 22:39), interrupt their prayers, and inform them they better sit up in the balcony with the other black folk. Richard and Absalom and the rest of the blacks walk out.

Rev. Allen Begins His Own Methodist Church

From then on, Richard begins to gather funds together to start his own Methodist Church. Absalom Jones eventually becomes a pastor at an Episcopal Church in town. Richard decides to stay with the Methodist Societies, stating:

"For the plain and simple gospel suits best for any people, for the unlearned can understand and the learned are sure to understand; and the reason that the Methodist is so successful in awakening and conversion of coloured people, the plain doctrine and having good discipline...I feel thankful that ever I heard a Methodist preach. We are beholden to the Methodists, under God, for the light of the Gospel we enjoy."[79]

Benjamin Rush (a signer of the Declaration of Independence) and other Philadelphians give money to build a church. This includes President George Washington who gives financially to this effort. Richard begins to search for a suitable piece of property.

In 1787, Richard founds the Free African Society which is a mutual aid society to help widows, orphans and the sick. Assistance is given to burying the dead for families who can not afford to do so. In 1790, Richard marries Flora whom he met at a Methodist class meeting at St. George's Church. Flora assists Richard in charitable work, supporting other black families in the community, and in raising funds for a new church.

Before Richard can build his new church, a Yellow Fever epidemic breaks out in Philadelphia in August 1793. The outbreak is so severe that thousands of citizens come down with the disease. Thousands of others flee the city. Government offices and businesses shut down.

Dr. Benjamin Rush organizes medical efforts to treat those affected by the fever. Little is known at the time what causes the illness. At one point only three doctors are left to treat all the patients. Dr. Rush asks Richard and his church people to assist in caring for the sick and to give help in burying the dead. Richard reaches out across Philadelphia to render assistance.

In 1794, Richard finds an old blacksmith shop which he buys and moves to Sixth and Lombard streets in Philadelphia. The shop is updated and remodeled. On July 29, Bishop Francis Asbury conducts the dedication and recognizes *The Blacksmith Shop Meeting House* as the first Black Methodist Society. Rev. John Dickins, from St. George's Church, prays at the dedication that this new meeting house be a bethel place for new souls. The name of the new church becomes Bethel Church. The name Bethel means a house of God and a gate to heaven. (Genesis 28:17).

On March 11, 1801, Flora Allen dies after a long illness. She and Richard do not have any children. Later that same year, Richard marries Sarah Bass who is a founding member of Bethel Church. Sarah and Richard will go on to have six children. Sarah becomes known for her kindness, virtue and becomes known as Mother Allen.

Rev. Allen Founds the African Methodist Episcopal Denomination

Richard and other black leaders in his church break away from oversight by St. George's Church and Annual Conference in 1816, and form their own separate African Methodist Episcopal denomination. This means Richard pays $10,125 to the Methodist Episcopal Church Conference for Bethel Church property to be free and separate from the conference.

In April 1816, the first General Conference meets at Bethel Church with representatives from other Black Methodist congregations in

Maryland, Delaware, New Jersey, and Pennsylvania. Richard is consecrated the first Bishop of the newly formed church.

Richard reminds his church members about bitterness and ill will toward others when he states:

"Let no rancor or ill-will lodge in your breast for any bad treatment you may have received from any. If you do, you transgress against God, who will not hold you guiltless. He will not suffer it even in His beloved people Israel; and you think He will allow it to us?"[80]

Loving his Savior more, Richard writes these words to describe his life in this world when entering the next:

"O crucified Jesus in whom I live, and without whom I die: mortify me in all sensual desires, inflame my heart with thy love, that I may no longer esteem the vanities of this world, but place my affections entirely upon thee. Let my last breath, when my soul shall leave my body, breathe forth love to thee, my God; I entered into this life without acknowledging thee, let me therefore finish it in loving thee: O let the last act of life to be love, remembering that God is love."[81]

****

But one thing I do: Forgetting what is behind and straining toward what is ahead, I press on toward the goal to win the prize for which God has called me heavenward in Christ Jesus. Philippians 3:13b-14.

John Quincy Adams 1767-1848

Lawyer, Diplomat, Abolitionist, State Senator, Secretary of State, Sixth President of the United States, Served in U.S. House of Representatives after serving as President

John Quincy is born on July 11, 1767 in Braintree (now Quincy) Massachusetts as the second child and first son of John and Abigail Adams. At the age of seven, he witnesses the Battle of Bunker Hill with his mother Abigail as they stand on a hillside behind their home. John Quincy says the images of the battle stay with him all of his life. After seeing the battle, Abigail has John Quincy promise her he will say the Lord's Prayer each morning when he gets out of bed. This he continues to do throughout his life.

When the schools close due to the war, Abigail takes command of John Quincy's education. She encourages him to read books from his father's library, which he does. Abigail calls on John Thaxter, a cousin who is studying law, to teach John Quincy mathematics and the sciences. At age ten, John Quincy is reading Shakespeare, daily newspapers, and the Bible.

John Quincy Travels to Europe with His Father

In 1778, John Adams is appointed as an emissary to France to seek aid for the Continental Army from the French. John takes his son John Quincy with him. John engages the ship's French doctor to teach his son to speak French during the voyage. John Quincy shows a natural talent for learning languages.

Once in Paris, John Adams finds a boarding school for John Quincy that is close enough he can spend Sundays with his son. School curriculum includes Latin, French, music, dancing, fencing and drawing. John Quincy in several weeks is able to speak passable French. This begins John Quincy's preparation for the many diplomatic posts he would hold throughout his life. He learns first-hand about diplomatic meetings and communications from his father and Ben Franklin who continues to represent America in

France at the time. French is the diplomatic language used across Europe. John Quincy begins writing his personal journal while he is at the Paris boarding school.

After a short trip home to Braintree after eleven months in France, John is again appointed this time as minister to France in 1779. John takes his sons John Quincy and Charles, and John Thaxter as their tutor with him.

John finds the French are stalling in completing any negotiations with the Americans so he decides to go to Holland. He enrolls John Quincy and Charles at the University of Leyden and finds lodging for them and John Thaxter. John finds the Dutch much more helpful in providing finances for the Continental Army.

John Quincy takes up his studies in Latin, Greek, and now learns to speak Dutch. John Quincy makes friends with Jean Luzac, a lawyer and editor of the leading Dutch newspaper. John Quincy introduces Luzac to his father who finds Luzac is Holland's leading advocate for giving aid to the Americans and recognizes America's right to independence.

John Quincy Goes to Russia to Translate for the American Minister

In 1781, Francis Dana is appointed the American minister to the court of Empress Catherine the Great in St. Petersburg, Russia. Dana does not speak French and has no way of conversing with the Russian Court. John Quincy at age fourteen goes along as Dana's secretary and translator. John Quincy's brother Charles returns to America.

In 1783, John Quincy rejoins his father in The Hague where John is now ambassador to Holland. John Quincy finishes up his studies at Leyden University and then returns to Massachusetts and begins his law studies at Harvard University. He graduates in 1787, is admitted to the Massachusetts Bar in 1790, and sets up his law office in Boston.

John Quincy Is Appointed U.S. Minister to Holland

In 1794, President George Washington appoints John Quincy as U.S. Minister to Holland on the basis that John Quincy has exquisite diplomatic skills and speaks Dutch. He asks his younger brother Thomas to go with him to Holland as an aide. Thomas agrees.

John Quincy is Appointed U.S. Minister to Prussia

In early 1796, John Quincy travels to London on a trip and visits the home of Joshua Johnson who is the American Consul. John Quincy meets Louisa Catherine Johnson, the second oldest daughter, and proposes to her on February 2, 1796. John Quincy and Louisa are married in 1797 and move to Prussia where John Quincy is appointed as U.S. Minister.

They will go on to have three sons who grow to adulthood and one daughter who dies as an infant.

New Year's Day 1800, begins a year of change for John Quincy. The night before he witnesses a young officer of the Prussian Court die suddenly at a ball and vows to begin reading the Bible every day which he does for the rest of his life. John Quincy comments on the beginning of a new century:

"I passed the period of transition between two centuries in communion with my soul and in prostration to the Being who directs the universe, with thanksgiving for his numerous blessings in the past times..."[82]

John Adams is not re-elected to the presidency in November of 1800. John Quincy is called home from diplomatic service and arrives in Philadelphia on June 17, 1801. John Quincy will go on to serve as a state senator of Massachusetts, and in 1804 is appointed as U.S. Minister to Russia.

John Quincy Appointed to Peace Commission

John Quincy watches the War of 1812 break out and follows developments from abroad. When the war ends, President Madison appoints John Quincy as the head of an American commission to negotiate a peace treaty with Great Britain in Ghent, Belgium. John Quincy is the most experienced American diplomat and authority on European politics at the time. He is able to get the wording of the peace treaty such that the United States is listed first as an equal with Great Britain. The United States begins an era of peace.

John Quincy Becomes Secretary of State

In 1817, President Monroe appoints John Quincy Secretary of State. John Quincy writes a prayer to God before he takes the oath of office:

"Thy gracious wisdom to fulfil, my constant aim incline; Grant my feeble, faltering will, the unerring strength of Thine."[83]

John Quincy immediately sets about organizing the State Department. He puts clerks to work cataloguing diplomatic correspondence and dispatches and starts a State Department Library. He responds to a mandate from Congress to report on Weights and Measures used in countries around the world. This report becomes the basis for the uniform weights and measures system of the United States. He sets standard protocol for all American diplomats abroad.

John Quincy enters into negotiations with British Lord Castlereagh whom he knows well from previous meetings in London as a diplomat. He is able for the first time to permanently fix the American-Canadian border by extending it along the forty-ninth parallel westward from the Great Lakes to the Rocky Mountains. John Quincy further informs the

British that America claims the mouth of the Columbia River, and fixes a ten year agreement that the British and Americans share the Oregon Territory which covers the present states of Oregon, Washington and western Idaho. This gives Americans access to the Pacific Ocean and a trade route to the Orient.

On February 22, 1821, John Quincy succeeds in an exchange of treaties with Spain. Spain gives up Florida and any claims on land west of the Sabine River, and sets the western boundaries of the Louisiana Purchase which opens up land to the summit of the Rocky Mountains. Upon signing the treaty with Spain, he makes a note in his journal:

"A watchful eye, a resolute...pose, a calm temper, and a favoring Providence will all be indispensable for the future as they have been in the past for the management of negotiation. May they not be found wanting."[84]

President Monroe further asks John Quincy to write up a policy statement for American land claims versus European land claims in the New World. This policy statement becomes known as the Monroe Doctrine.

John Quincy Is Elected the Sixth President of the United States

John Quincy Adams is elected the sixth President of the United States on February 9, 1825. At the end of the day after being sworn in, he writes in his journal:

"I closed the day as it had begun with Thanksgiving to God for all his mercies and favors past, and with prayers for the continuance of them to my Country and to myself and to mine."[85]

On July 4, 1837, John Quincy gives an address in Newport, Massachusetts to commemorate the sixty-first birthday of the Declaration of Independence at the largest meeting place in town, the First Presbyterian Church. John Quincy exclaims,

"Is it not in the chain of human events, the birth of a nation is indissolubly linked with the birthday of the Savior? The Declaration of Independence laid the cornerstone of human government upon the first precepts of Christianity."[86]

On the two hundred anniversary of the First Congregational Church in Quincy, Massachusetts a hymn entitled, *How Swift Alas the Moments Fly*, is sung to words written by John Quincy. In these words we find John Quincy summing up his view of life.

"Then pilgrim, let thy joys and tears on time no longer lean; But henceforth all thy hopes and fears from earth's affections wean; To God let votive accents arise; with truth, with virtue, live; So all the bliss that Time denies, Eternity shall give."[87]

****

Chapter Four Questions for Reflection

1. Which First Amendment right does Haym Salomon state is the most important? Do you agree with Haym that is the most important over all other freedoms?
2. What does Noah Webster say is the cause of all the miseries and evils that men and women suffer in society? What is moral virtue? Where does moral virtue come from? What does Noah Webster say about prayer? Do you agree? Why or why not?
3. Rev. Richard Allen writes that those unjustly wronged are not to let rancor or deep seated ill will arise from mistreatment. He states to do so is a transgression against God. Do you agree? Why or why not? Rev. Allen states working with God to bring freedom to people is what brings true lasting freedom. Do you agree? Why or why not?
4. What does John Quincy Adams say is the cornerstone of the Declaration of Independence? Where does John Quincy Adams say one receives virtue and truth to live his or her life? What might we as Americans need to thank God for? Why might we citizens of the United States need to rely upon God for the success of not only our personal lives, but also the success of our nation?

Endnotes

Chapter One—-Trust in God

1. Lossing, B.J. *Signers of the Declaration of Independence.* Samuel Adams to British Governor Gage, 1774, 35.
2. Cushing, H. ed. *Writings of Samuel Adams.* Samuel Adams to Andrew Elton Wells, July 25, 1774, Kindle Edition, 3:160.
3. *Ibid.*, Samuel Adams to Betsy Adams, June 16, 1775, 3:236.
4. *Ibid.*, Samuel Adams to Betsy Adams, June 28, 1775, 3:239-240.
5. *Ibid.*, Samuel Adams to Betsy Adams, October 20, 1775, 3:248.
6. *Ibid.*, Samuel Adams to Betsy Adams, November 7, 1776, 3:253.
7. *Ibid.*, Samuel Adams to John Adams, September 16, 1776, 3:325.
8. Abigail Adams to John Adams, June 18-20, 1775. *Adams Family Papers: Electronic Archive.* Massachusetts Historical Society, http://www.masshist.org/digitaladams.
9. *Ibid.*
10. *Ibid.,* Abigail Adams to John Adams, June 25, 1775.
11. *Ibid.*, Abigail Adams to John Adams, June 17, 1775.
12. *Ibid.*
13. Franklin, B. *Memoirs of Benjamin Franklin*, Kindle Edition, 1:1234.

14. *Ibid.*, 1:1616-1625.

15. *Ibid.*, 1:3679-3697.

16. Rush, B. *A Memorial Containing Travels Through Life or Sundry Incidents in the Life of Benjamin Rush*, 105.

17. *Ibid.*, 59.

18. Rush, B. *Essays, Literary, Moral and Philosophical*, 8-9.

19. *Ibid.*, 70.

20. *Ibid.*, 8-9.

Chapter Two—-Hope in God

21. Greene, G.W. *Life of Nathanael Greene*. Nathanael Greene to his wife Kitty, 1:106-107.

22. *Ibid.*, Nathanael Greene to his wife Kitty, 1:316-317.

23. *Ibid.*, Nathanael Greene to his wife Kitty, 2:232.

24. Thayer, T. *Nathanael Greene Strategist of the American Revolution*. Nathanael Greene to Governor Cooke, January 10, 1777, 147.

25. Pierson, H. *Jefferson at Monticello: The Private Life of Thomas Jefferson*. Captain Edmund Bacon's narrative to Rev. Pierson, Kindle Edition, 1088.

26. Jefferson, T. *Rough Draft of the Declaration of Independence*, June 1776. Thomas Jefferson Papers at the Library of Congress, 1651-1827, image 545-547.

27. Jefferson, T. *Declaration of Independence*, July 4, 1776. Thomas Jefferson Papers at the Library of Congress, 1651-1827, image 556-559.

28. Jefferson, T. *First Inaugural Address*, March 4, 1801. Thomas Jefferson Papers at the Library of Congress, Series 1, General Correspondence 1651-1827, image 67.

29. Witherspoon, J. *Works of John Witherspoon,* Vol.1, 98.

30. *Ibid.*, Vol. 9, 94.
31. *Ibid.*, 104.
32. *Ibid.*, Vol. 5, 202-203.
33. Pattison, E., "The Life and Character of Richard Bassett," Vol. 29, 14, narrative of Richard Bassett preaching to a Methodist Society meeting. And in *Founders of Freedom in America*, p. 46.
34. *Ibid.*, 13. Bishop Francis Asbury note in his journal about Richard Bassett.
35. Wharton, A. *Women of Colonial and Revolutionary Times: Martha Washington*. Martha Washington to Edward Pendleton, Kindle Edition, 1031.
36. *Ibid.*
37. Johnson, W. *George Washington the Christian*. Dorothy Dudley's diary notes on attending church with Martha and General Washington New Year's Day, January 1, 1776, Kindle Edition, 775.
38 . Wharton, A. *Women of Colonial and Revolutionary Times: Martha Washington.* Mrs. Westlake identified in 1898 edition as the source of narrative about Martha Washington, Kindle Edition, 1495.
39. *Ibid.*, Martha Washington in a letter from Cambridge to her sister, Kindle Edition, 1278.
40. Greene, G.W. *Life of Nathanael Greene.* Nathanael Greene to his wife Kitty, 1:356-357.
41. Custis, G.W. *Recollections and Private Memoirs of Washington.* Narrative of author on General Washington, Kindle Edition, 3202-3226.
42. Johnson, W. George *Washington the Christian.* Martha Washington in a letter to a distant relative, Kindle Edition, 672.

Chapter Three—-Faith in God

43. Fitzpatrick, J. ed. *The Writings of George Washington from the Original Manuscript Sources, Vol. 1.* George Washington to Augustine Washington, July 8, 1755. Edited 1784.
44. Custis, G.W. *Recollections and Private Memoirs of Washington.* Author's narrative about General Washington, Kindle Edition, 389.
45. Fitzpatrick, J. ed. *The Writings of George Washington from the Original Manuscript Sources, Vol. 3.* George Washington to Martha Washington, June 18, 1775.
46. *Ibid.*, George Washington's General Orders, July 16, 1775.
47. *Ibid., Vol. 5.* George Washington's General Orders, July 2, 1775.
48. *Ibid.*, George Washington's General Orders, July 9, 1776.
49. *Ibid., Vol. 11.* George Washington's General Orders, May 2, 1778.
50. Washington, G. *First Inaugural Address*, April 30, 1789. George Washington's Papers at Library of Congress,1741-1799. Series 2, Letterbooks, image 24-40.
51. Fitzpatrick, J. ed. *The Writings of George Washington from the Original Manuscript Sources, Vol. 30.* President Washington's Thanksgiving Proclamation, October 3, 1789.
52. *Ibid, Vol. 36.* George Washington to Lawrence Lewis, 1797.
53. Johnson, W. *George Washington the Christian.* Words of prayer in George Washington's handwriting, Kindle Edition, 191-202.
54. John Adams to Abigail Adams, August 28, 1774. *Adams Family Papers: Electronic Archive.* Massachusetts Historical Society. http://masshist.org/digitaladams.
55. *Ibid.*, John Adams to Abigail Adams, July 7, 1775.
56. *Ibid.*, John Adams to Abigail Adams, July 3, 1776.
57. *Ibid.*

58. *Ibid.*, John Adams to Abigail Adams, November 2, 1800.

59. *Annals of Congress*, Journal of the Senate, Vol. 2, Appendix, March 4, 1797, 398-401. *First Inaugural Address* of President John Adams.

60. Rowland, K. *Life and Correspondence of Charles Carroll of Carrollton, Vol. 2*, 321.

61. Leonard, L. *Life of Charles Carroll of Carrollton*. Writing of Charles Carroll about the fiftieth anniversary of the signing of the Declaration of Independence, 256-257.

62. Gay, S. *James Madison*. James Madison to Thomas Jefferson, 1787, Kindle Edition, 1114.

63. *Ibid.*, Virginia Bill of Rights, Kindle Edition, 689.

64. *Annals of Congress*, Journal of the Senate, Vol. 4, March 4, 1809, 366-367. *First Inaugural Address* of President James Madison.

65. Clark, A. *The Selected Letters of Dolley Payne Madison.* Dolley to her sister Lucy Todd, Kindle Edition, 2919.

66. *Ibid.*, Kindle Edition, 2908.

67. *Annals of Congress*, March 4, 1815, Appendix 16, 764. President Madison's Day of Thanksgiving Proclamation.

68. *Ibid*, Congress' proclamation for a Day of Thanksgiving.

Chapter Four—Love in God

69. Baron, H. *Haym Salomon: Immigrant and Financier of the American Revolution*, 45.

70. *Ibid.*, 53.

71. Webster, N. "A Moral Catechism." *The American Spelling Book: Containing the Rudiments of the English Language, for Use of Schools in the United States*, 167.

72. Webster, N. *The Elementary Spelling Book Being an Improvement on the American Spelling Book*, 69, 75.
73. Webster, N. *History of the United States*, 339.
74. *Ibid.*, 300.
75 .Ford, E. *Notes on the Life of Noah Webster, Vol. 2*. Prayer of Noah Webster, 198-199.
76. Allen, R. *The Life Experience, and Gospel Labors of the Rt. Rev. Richard Allen*, 6.
77. *Ibid.,* 5.
78. *Ibid.*, 7.
79. *Ibid.*, 16-17.
80. *Ibid.*, 48.
81. *Ibid.*, 28.
82. John Quincy Adams' diary entry for December 31, 1800, 314. *Diaries of John Quincy Adams: A Digital Collection.* Massachusetts Historical Society. http://www.masshist.org/jqdiaries.
83. *Ibid.*, John Quincy Adams' diary entry for September 21, 1817, 276.
84. *Ibid.*, John Quincy Adams' diary entry for February 22, 1819, 46.
85. *Ibid.*, John Quincy Adams' diary entry for February 9, 1825, 104.
86. Adams, JQ. *An Oration Delivered Before the Inhabitants of the Town of Newburyport, at Their Request on the Sixty-First Anniversary of the Declaration of Independence, July 4, 1837*, 5-6.
87. Adams, JQ. *Poems of Religion and Society*, Kindle Edition, 714.

Bibliography

1. Adams, John and Abigail. *Adams Family Papers. An Electronic Archive*. Massachusetts Historical Society. http://www.masshist.org/digitaladams.
2. Adams, John Quincy. *Diaries of John Quincy Adams: A Digital Collection.* Massachusetts Historical Society. http://masshist.org/jqadiaries.
3. Adams, John Quincy. (1853) *Poems of Religion and Society.* Auburn: Derby and Miller. Kindle Edition, 2010. Citation from Kindle edition.
4. Adams, John Quincy (1837) *An Oration, Delivered Before the Inhabitants of the Town of Newburyport at Their Request on the Sixty-First Anniversary of the Declaration of Independence, July 4, 1837.* Newburyport, Mass: Morse and Brewster. Nabu Public Domain Reprints, 2010. Citation from Nabu edition.
5. Allen, Richard. (1833) *The Life Experience and Gospel Labors of the Rt. Reverend Richard Allen.* Documenting the American South. University Library. The University of North Carolina at Chapel Hill, 2004. http://docusouth.unc.edu/neh/allen/allen.hmtl.
6. Allen, Thomas B. *George Washington, Spymaster: How the Americans Outspied the British and Won the Revolutionary War.* Washington, D.C.: National Geographic, 2004.

7. *Annals of Congress.* Journal of the Senate, Vol 2. Appendix, March 4, 1797. A New Century of Lawmaking for a New Nation: U.S. Congressional Documents and Debates 1774-1875.
8. *Annals of Congress.* Journal of the Senate. Vol. 4, March 4, 1809. A New Century of Lawmaking for a New Nation: U.S. Congressional Documents and Debates, 1774-1875.
9. *Annals of Congress.* March 4, 1815. Appendix 16. A New Century of Lawmaking for a New Nation: U.S. Congressional Documents and Debates, 1774-1875.
10. Baron, H.S. (1929) *Haym Salomon: Immigrant and Financier of the American Revolution.* New York: Bloch Publishing. Kessinger Legacy Reprints, 2010. Citations from Kessinger edition.
11. Boyer, Marilyn. *For You They Signed.* Green Forest, Arkansas: Master Books, 2009.
12. Clark, Allen C. (1914) *Life and Letters of Dolley Madison.* Washington, D.C.: Press of W.F. Roberts Company. Kindle Edition, 2014. Citations from Kindle edition.
13. Cushing, Harry Alonzo, ed. (1904-1908) *The Writings of Samuel Adams.* New York: G.P. Putnam's Sons. Kindle Edition, 2011-2012. Citations from Kindle edition.
14. Custis, George Washington Parke. (1859) *Private Recollections and Memoirs of Washington.* Washington, D.C.: William H. Moore. Kindle Edition, 2012. Citations from Kindle edition.
15. Fitzpatrick, John C. ed. *The Writings of George Washington from the Original Manuscript Sources, 1745-1799.* National Digital Library Program. Library of Congress, Electronic Version, 1997. U.S. Govt. Print Office, 1931-1944.

16. Ford, Emily E. Fowler. (1912) *Notes on the Life of Noah Webster, Vol. 2.* New York: Privately Published. Nabu Public Domain Reprints, 2010. Citations from Nabu edition.
17. Franklin, Benjamin. (1839) *Memoirs of Benjamin Franklin.* New York: Harper & Publishers. Kindle Edition, 2011-2012. Citations from Kindle edition.
18. Gay, Syndey H. (1892) *James Madison.* Boston: Houghton and Mifflin. Kindle Edition 2012. Citations from Kindle edition.
19. Greene, George Washington (1867) *Life of Nathanael Greene, Vol. 1.* New York: G.P. Putnam's Sons. (1871) *Vol. 2.* New York: Hurd and Houghton. Nabu Public Domain Reprints, 2010. Citations from Nabu edition.
20. Harrell, David Erwin, et al. *Unto a Good Land: A History of the American People.* Grand Rapids, Michigan: William B. Eerdmans Publishing Company, 2005.
21. Jefferson, Thomas. *Rough Draft of the Declaration of Independence,* June 1776. Thomas Jefferson Papers at the Library of Congress, Series 1. General Correspondence, 1651-1827, image 545-547. http://hdl.loc.gov.mss/mtjbib000516.
22. Jefferson, Thomas. *Declaration of Independence.* Thomas Jefferson Papers at the Library of Congress, Series 1. General Correspondence. 1651-1827. Image 556-559. http://hdl.loc.gov.mss/mjtibib000159.
23. Jefferson, Thomas. *First Inaugural Address,* March 4, 1801. Thomas Jefferson Papers at Library of Congress, Series 1. General Correspondence, 1651-1827, image 67. http://hdl.loc.gov.mss/mjtibib009728.
24. Johnson, William J. (1919) *George Washington the Christian.* New York: Abingdon Press. Kindle Edition, 2013. Citations from Kindle edition.

25. Leonard, Lewis A. (1918) *A Life of Charles Carroll of Carrollton.* New York: Moffat, Yard and Company. Nabu Public Domain Reprints, 2010. Citations from Nabu edition.
26. Lossing, B.J. (1866) *Biographical Sketches of the Signers of the Declaration of Independence.* Nabu Public Domain Reprints, 2010. Citations from Nabu edition.
27. Pattison, Robert E. (1900) "The Life and Character of Richard Bassett," Vol. 29, 3-19. Historical Society of Delaware: Wilmington. Reprint of narrative dialogue in Whitney, D. *Founders of Freedom in America*, 1965. Citations from both editions.
28. Pierson, Rev. Hamilton. (1862) *Jefferson at Monticello: The Private Life of Thomas Jefferson.* New York: Charles Scribner & Sons. Kindle Edition, 2010. Citations from Kindle edition.
29. Peters, Madison C. (1911) *Haym Salomon Financier of the Revolution.* New York: The Trow Press. Kindle Edition, 2014.
30. Rowland, Kate Mason. (1898) *Life and Correspondence of Charles Carroll of Carrollton. Vol. 2.* New York: G.P. Putnam's Sons. Kessinger Legacy Reprints, 2010. Citation from Kessinger edition.
31. Rush, Benjamin. (1905) *A Memorial Containing Travels Through Life or Sundry Incidents in the Life of Dr. Benjamin Rush, Born Dec. 24, 1745, Died, April 19, 1813.* Published Privately by Louis Biddle in Philadelphia. Nabu Public Domain Reprints, 2010. Citations from Nabu edition.
32. Rush, Benjamin. (1806) *Essays, Literary, Moral and Philosophical.* Philadelphia: Thomas and William Bradford. Kessinger Legacy Reprints, 2010. Citations from Kessinger edition.
33. Thayer, Theodore. (1960) *Nathanael Greene Strategist of the American Revolution.* New York: Twayne Publishers. Nabu Public Domain Reprints, 2010. Citation from both editions.

34. Washington, George. *First Inaugural Address,* April 30, 1789. George Washington Papers at the Library of Congress 1741-1799. Series 2, Letterbox 25, image 8.
35. Webster, Noah. (1822) "A Moral Catechism." *The American Spelling Book: Containing the Rudiments of the English Language for the Use of Schools in the United States.* Albany: Websters and Skinners. Nabu Public Domain Reprints, 2010. Citations from Nabu edition.
36. Webster, Noah. (1908) *The Elementary Spelling Book, Being an Improvement on the American Spelling Book.* New York: American Book Company. Nabu Public Domain Reprints, 2011. Citations from both editions.
37. Webster, Noah. (1832) *History of the United States: To Which is Prefixed a Brief Historical Account of Our English Ancestors, from the Dispersion of Babel to Their Migration to America, and the Conquest of South America, By the Spaniards.* New Haven: Durrie & Peck. Nabu Public Domain Reprints, 2010. Citations from Nabu edition.
38. Wharton, Anne Hollingsworth. (1897) *Women of Colonial and Revolutionary Times: Martha Washington.* New York: Charles Scribner's Sons. Kindle Edition, 2014. Citations from Kindle edition.
39. Whitney, David C. ed. *Founders of Freedom in America: Lives of the Men Who Signed the Constitution of the United States and So Helped to Establish the United States of America.* Chicago: J.G. Ferguson Publishing Company, 1965.
40. Wigger, John H. "Holy-Knock Em-Down Preachers: The Common Methodist Circuit Rider Transformed American Christianity." *Christian History,* Issue 45 (1995) Vol. XIV, 22-25.
41. Witherspoon, John. (1804-1805) *The Works of John Witherspoon, D.D.* Edinburgh: Ogle And Aikmen, J. Pillans, J. Richtie, J. Turnbull. Nabu Public Domain Reprints, 2012. Citations from Nabu edition.

42. Wright, Robert K. and MacGreagor, Morris J. *Soldiers-Statesman of the Constitution.* Washington, D.C.: Center for Military History, United States Army, 1987.

CPSIA information can be obtained
at www.ICGtesting.com
Printed in the USA
FSOW01n1447010916
24498FS

9 781498 448376